ANIMA CHRISTI

MOTHER MARY FRANCIS, P.C.C.

ANIMA CHRISTI

Soul of Christ

IGNATIUS PRESS   SAN FRANCISCO

Cover art: *The Deposition* (detail)
Fra Angelico
Museo San Marco, Florence, Italy
Erich Lessing/Art Resource, New York

Cover design by Roxanne Mei Lum

To the memory of
God's gallant Knight,
Dr. Emmit Jennings

CONTENTS

PREFACE

Anima Christi is a favorite prayer of mine, one I have prayed daily since the age of thirteen, as a sophomore in high school. I discovered myself to be in very good company when I learned that Pope Pius XII also prayed the *Anima Christi* each morning after Holy Communion. But I take up this prayer as a theme to be shared, not because it is a cherished devotion of mine, but because there is such a wealth of theology and devotion in it for the enrichment of our thought and the deepening of our understanding of Christology. Our stock of vocal prayers tends to decrease as we become more and more absorbed in the liturgical prayer of the Church, which blends into our most private prayer so as to leave no longer any sign of boundary. Liturgical communal prayer and the deepest private prayer flow in and out of each other. And we develop certain "code expressions" in our very private life of love with God. Perhaps little aspirations or fragments of aspirations. It is not to propose the adding of a vocal prayer to anyone's own elected store that I want to reflect on the *Anima Christi*, but to explore its immense riches, which each can invest as God leads him.

I

ANIMA CHRISTI, SANCTIFICA ME

Soul of Christ, sanctify me

WHAT DO WE MEAN BY *"anima Christi"*? What idea are we conveying when we speak of the "soul of Christ"? Although we would not articulate it even to ourselves in words so crude, is it not true that we can tend to lapse into some vague quasi-concept of the soul of Christ as being somehow the Divinity infused into a human body? This is not the soul of Christ. His was a created human soul. And here we enter into a realm of great mystery. We are speaking of a Divine Person, the Son of God. And we readily accept in faith a fact that, of course, we can never of ourselves comprehend: that this Divine Person had a created human body that began life in the womb of the Virgin Mary solely by the overshadowing of the Holy Spirit and without intervention of man. We follow the human growth of the Son of God through the Scriptures, as Jesus is born, learns to walk and to speak, questions, comprehends, matures, passes through all the phases of human growth to full manhood, and dies a human death after enduring human suffering and human temptations. This Divine Person is God, yet this human body was created. Agreed, surely. Yet doubtless our human minds, limited by reason of our humanity, need a bit more time and a great deal more effort to absorb the fact that the human soul of Christ was also created. He entered into humanity perfectly equipped and without any of our infirmities of original sin, with a human mind of such depth as we cannot gauge, a human body complete in a perfection beyond that of any other human creature walking about in a body, an exquisitely perfect human nervous system, a supreme sensitiveness of spirit, emotions tuned like a Stradivarius and beyond it, and human preferences and non-preferences. It is rather delightful to think that Jesus may have found beans more agreeable than corn, liked bananas better than oranges. But that he had a human soul—our thinking tends to come to a grinding halt before this.

Anima is the Latin root of many English words. We speak of a person as being animated. We say, "She has such an animated countenance", and everyone knows what we mean. Her face is very much "alive". Even slang has something to tell us when it offers the expression "dead pan". We know what that means, too. An animated person does not have a dead face, but a face full of life. We speak of a person's animated way of speaking, of an animated gait or animated gestures. And by all of these we mean: life! If we are trying to help a person in reading aloud or directing a person in a play, we may well have occasion to say: "Oh, show more animation. Be more alive!" And we speak of inanimate creation, which is literally creation without the vital life principle. Rocks and stones are part of the inanimate creation of God. Plants already enter into animate creation, which involves the life principle of beginning, growth, death. And animals (it is tempting to digress on the noun here!) testify by their very name that they are a higher part of animate creation. Then we ascend to man, with his exalted, created life-principle given to him by the creating Father, given to each one of us, given to Christ. It is to this created soul of Christ that we cry out, "Make me holy!—sanctify me!" "*Anima Christi, sanctifica me.*" In him is the source of life, of the animation that makes it possible for us to be completely alive in holiness.

Each of us has his own created animating principle, his particular soul created by the Father. Unlike Christ, we are in need of redemption, of the continual sanctification of our spirit. But our vital life principle, the animating principle, is like Christ's soul in being the creation of the Father and in having the same ministering faculties: memory, imagination, intellect, will, and in being served by the senses.

We know only too well that our vital animating principle, our soul, is often ill served by its ministering, subservient faculties. Christ's soul was all-perfect, and its ministering human faculties served it perfectly. It is to the soul of Christ that we must, therefore, look for our sanctification. We shall not find it in our own animating principle, so wounded by original sin and so weakened again and again by actual sin. In Christ's soul, never subject to original sin, never damaged in the slightest way by actual sin, but "tempted as we are, yet without sinning" (Heb 4:15), we have that pure force of the one animating principle in which we can be made holy.

Let us look at some of the ministering faculties of Christ's soul. He had a memory, and he made human decisions about how to use his memory. We need strength to make right decisions, a strength not to be found in our weakened life principle but only in the soul of Christ. Many incidents in the life of Christ as recorded in the Gospels show us the choices he made about how to use his memory.

We know so well the Gospel account of the ten lepers made clean, only one of whom returns to thank Christ. How much is revealed in this instance of the human heart of Christ and the human soul of Christ. He let us know that he was hurt by ingratitude. "Were not ten made clean? Where are the nine? Was no one found to return and give praise to God except this foreigner?" (Lk 17:17). We can say that Christ's memory was assaulted by the sorrow evoked in him by the ingratitude of the nine. But he chose not to "remember" after that one revelatory cry of his human heart, surely enough to break the ungrateful hearts of us all. He let us know how he felt and about the struggle with the hurt of his human heart; but then he made a human decision not to "remember" by being very slow to grant his favors again. Or, in our cramped language: he did not decide that he would really think twice before he worked another miracle for this ungrateful mass of mankind. Instead, he chose to remember that one was grateful. We need to remember that a human Jesus suffered many temptations and needed to offer much human resistance and make multiple human choices. It was not just a matter of the initial three classic temptations (Lk 4:3–13), but a lifelong affair.

We find decisions like that quite difficult sometimes. It is so easy to remember the hurt, the misunderstanding, so tempting to rehearse to ourselves the ingratitudes. Christ elected to remember what would humanly enable him to go on doing good. He did not allow his memory to enfeeble his soul but humanly disciplined his human mind to serve his human soul. And there was Peter, with "saint" not quite yet prefixed to his name. When Jesus, after his Resurrection, asked the famous triple question, was he not telling us

15

what he would choose to remember about Peter? He gave his poor, weak, but so loving disciple, Peter, the opportunity to present him with what he would choose to remember. Jesus could have remembered only the denials. He chose to remember the love— and gave us our first pope.

There is another ministering faculty to the soul of Christ: his human imagination. One must not demote the imagination to a kind of perverted faculty of the soul. True, Saint Teresa of Jesus calls the imagination "that crazy woman in the house". And we know what she means. Certainly, if we allow the imagination to wander about undirected, it can be just like that: a crazed woman wandering in the house of our life and adept at creating havoc and useless suffering. But the imagination per se is a glorious faculty. It is our inbuilt television created by God long before man ever thought of throwing images on a screen. Man is always so far behind God. So, yes, the imagination is a marvelous creation, but one that cannot be allowed to overpower the soul. It has to be led and disciplined into subservience, not as a chained chattel of the soul, but as a good servant.

Imagination is particularly strong in some persons, and the suffering it can cause to them can likewise be a channel of suffering to others in whom it is less strong. This still does not mean that there is anything wrong or base about imagination as such. An article about the bombing of a convent in a certain country told of the chaplain's trying to evacuate the nuns, with chaos all about him. The bricks were falling, the glass was flying. Would he make it? Could he save the nuns? And the writer said, with a nice literary turn, "It was certainly not a good hour in which to have a strong imagination. And, unfortunately, the chaplain was a poet!" Christ also was a poet, the like of whom we shall never hear again. And so his imagination, being perfect, presented to him possibilities in fuller color than any of ours ever will. In the Garden of Gethsemane, what his imagination presented to him of the sufferings to come could have been and nearly was completely overpowering, except that the soul of Christ made of that imagination a servant to itself. The full-color screen of what was coming, what might be, what the physical sufferings would feel like, look like, the "uselessness" of it for how many souls . . . this had to have been on the screen of Christ's all-perfect imagination. Keeping that imagination what it was created to be, the good servant of the human soul, was part of his saying: "Not my will, but yours, be done" (Lk 22:42).

All that memory told him, in that climactic hour, of what was in the heart of man as he had humanly discovered it—"He . . . knew what was in man" (Jn 2:25)—all that his imagination gave him in full color of what was to be, could be, or might be, his human intelligence took, presenting the findings of both faculties to his human will in an all-perfect and, therefore, because all-perfect, an all-suffering act. The created intelligence of Christ took the records of memory and the proposals of imagination and all that came to it through his created senses, and made conclusions. It heard their case, accepting the testimony of the senses of the man, Christ, and the ministering faculties of his created soul, and offered its conclusions about their findings to the supreme faculty of Christ's soul, his will. And the all-perfect will of Christ responded, though not without struggle, to decide his course. "Not my will, but yours, be done, O Father."

Our weakened and damaged soul, yet so beautiful and glorious and full of potential for eternal perfection, must find the strength to actuate its potential, not in itself, but in Christ. The apostle says, "Have this mind among yourselves, which was in Christ Jesus" (Phil 2:5). It is not that we abdicate our own principle of soul, our own mind, but that the mind of Christ takes possession of ours. Thus the apostle testifies that his own humanity has been perfected in the soul of Christ, that he has made the soul of Christ the animating principle of his own life: "It is no longer I who live, but Christ who lives in me" (Gal 2:20). Perfect human fulfillment is to allow one's self to be completely taken over by Christ, to deliver one's self to the sanctifying power of the soul of Christ, the *anima Christi.* It is to permit the perfect and unblemished animating principle of the created Christ to become my own. Therefore, when we speak of an animated person, in the loftiest spiritual sense we would mean a Christlike person. The more Christlike we are, the more animated we are in the basic etymological sense of the word. We are progressively "dead" insofar as we do not live in Christ. To be animated in this exalted sense is to be Christlike; to be more animated is to be more Christlike; to be totally animated is to live now, not I, but "Christ who lives in me".

When the apostle says, "Have this mind among yourselves, which was in Christ Jesus", what does he tell us that mind was? Does he present us with some dizzying galaxies of speculation? Does he tell us of things that belong in the third heaven, as he said in another place, things not to be understood in the language of men? What is the mind of Christ? It is to be totally emptied out in the service of the Father. This was the decision of our Lord. "Though he was in the form of God . . . [he] emptied himself, taking the form of a servant" (Phil 2:6–7). He poured himself out. That is what the Scriptures tell us is the mind of Christ, the soul of Christ, the principle of the human life of Christ. And so, when we pray: "*Anima Christi, sanctifica me*", we are indeed making a very bold and dangerous prayer, a tremendously exacting prayer. We are saying that we want to be emptied out, to experience our own kenosis as Christ experienced his, totally given, totally spent. "Soul of Christ, sanctify me." It will not be painless. No passion ever was.

II

CORPUS CHRISTI, SALVA ME

Body of Christ, save me

I<small>F WE MUST NOT ALLOW OURSELVES</small> to drift into vague conjectures or to rest content with nebulous concepts about the soul or the mind of Christ, as though this were the Divinity set down in the created human body as into some kind of cabinet, neither should we, however unwittingly, seek to disengage the body from the soul. In this inspired prayer, *Anima Christi*, beloved of so many saints, we see an immediate progression. It is not as though we are to be concerned only with the soul of Christ, agreeing that he had to have a body to get about in, a kind of second-class instrument necessary for divine locomotion as man and for carrying out the various enterprises of human existence. To guard against any such lowly concept of our own body (for that concept depends upon our concept of the body of Christ), the prayer proceeds directly from "*anima Christi*" to "*corpus Christi*".

"Body of Christ, save me!" we pray. That sets us back on our mental heels a bit. What do we mean—body, save me? Was it not the soul that saved us? Again, there are depths to plumb. The Church, in approving and indulgencing this prayer, gives us an advanced course in theology.

Our bodies are so noble. The infamous carnal sinners of history are, not those who loved their bodies too much, but those who loved their bodies too little. They are those who failed to respect or perhaps even to understand the dignity of that masterpiece of the Father, the human body. It is a creation so marvelous that the Father did not hesitate to give it to his own divine, eternal, infinite, all-comprehensive expression of himself in the Incarnation of the Son, in the same way that it is given to us and with the same senses and faculties possessed by our own bodies. The Father manifestly did not think this unbecoming. No, his own expression of himself, his Divine Logos, would become incarnate in a human body, brother to our own human bodies.

What seems clear in this prayer, "Body of Christ, save me", is not what might ordinarily come first to our minds (which is certainly a glorious consideration, to be sure): the Blessed Sacrament. Indeed, in this way "*Corpus Christi*", the Body of Christ, does save me. But there is also a revelation here about our own bodies as they are meant to be and which they can be only through the body of Christ, who is himself "the first-born of all creation" (Col 1:15) and whose created body was the perfect partner of his created soul.

A lowly estimate of our bodies results in our becoming prey to all manner of sins. When we consider the body only a necessary adjunct so that the soul can get about, we do our body a great dishonor. Conversely, when we hold the body as supreme, we likewise do it a great injustice and so, again, a dishonor. Body and soul are co-related, coordinated from the act of creation onward. Both will endure. True, the human body will fall into dust in the burial vault, but it will be resurrected in glory for eternity. We shall have glorified bodies in eternity; we shall not be disembodied spirits. We hope to see there the Jesus who shows to his Father the glorified wounds of his human body.

The body is ordained for ultimate glorification, and the very act of its decay in the tomb is the fulfillment of the penitential curse laid upon it in Eden. One might say that decomposition is the protest of the body at being temporarily parted from the soul, a protest appropriate in its very horror for manifesting what such a disassociation really is. We recognize the horror of the grave easily enough. Do we likewise recognize the horrors we create in life when we do not allow the body to act with the soul, to be served by the soul, and in its turn to serve the soul? The body must be taught that the soul is its animating principle.

When the body has desires that go beyond what the soul, that animating principle of the body, knows to be rightful boundaries, it must be admonished by the soul, by the mind. If the body desires more food than it needs, it has to be persuaded by the soul to curb those desires. Or if the body seeks repose that extends beyond, perhaps even far beyond, what is sufficient, into self-indulgent sloth, it must be admonished and disciplined. However, as the soul directs, educates, and admonishes the body, so does the body need in its turn sometimes to admonish the spirit. We are an integrity of body and soul, one human being. And the body expresses its own feelings through the faculties of mind and heart. This is evident enough.

The body beholds something that makes it fearful, and there are bodily reactions: the heart begins to pound, sometimes sweat gathers on the palms, the knees tremble, perhaps the muscles twitch and quiver. But there are also reactions within the incorporeal faculties themselves. For instance, a body subject to long and arduous strain will be accompanied in its duress by a tired mind. The intelligence will not be able to function as it ordinarily would.

Again, the incorporeal network of emotions are affected. If one is fatigued beyond a certain point, it is not possible to react to situations with emotional élan except in a very artificial and even damaging way. When a person has been ill for a long time, the faculties of the mind ordinarily also experience a kind of languor. Nor can we pray when the body is totally exhausted. We could go on multiplying examples. These are assuredly very profound, if obvious, considerations going in both directions. When there is a disappointment of hopes, the body becomes dispirited—a very precise expression. Lacking in spirit, it is not quite a body, so to speak.

Surely all of us have experienced that when we suffer disappointment in another's reaction or lack of response, we feel physically tired. On the other hand, when we are privileged to see another sincerely confronting the truth, to witness a truly humble reaction, to behold a real striving for holiness, our very body becomes animated. We are no longer tired, even though work might have left us so. Reserves of strength come surging up in us. Body and soul act and interact. The incorporeal faculties admonish the body; but the body also in its way admonishes the faculties of mind and spirit.

A tired body counsels the mind: "Stop working now. Let us rest together." And we know what happens when the mind refuses to follow the direction of the body. A very fatigued body can lie awake all night long because the mind says, "No, I will keep on thinking", when the body has said, "It's time to stop now and for us to go to sleep together." Body and soul cannot sleep apart, as least not in proper and healthful cofunctioning.

Indeed, it is the body of Christ in the Blessed Sacrament that saves us. But it is also the body of Christ in his human functioning, during the historical period of his corporeal activity upon this earth, when his body perfectly served his soul and his animating principle perfectly coordinated its activity with his body, that saves us. We do not see in ourselves or of ourselves these perfect coordinations. Rather, we know how often we are tossed about by our lack of coordination. The soul says to the body, "Do not pass this boundary", and the body replies, "I will!" The body wishes to and often enough does disobey the incorporeal faculties.

It is only in Christ, the perfect man, the firstborn of all creation, that we see the perfect functioning of the body. And so it is his body that will save us, that will show us how to be whole. What does *salva* mean? Save us, make us whole. Salvation is wholeness of life, just as sanity is wholeness of mind. There is a basic shared root. *Salvatus*, saved. *Sanatus*, made whole. We are saved when we are whole beyond any further assault. And Christ was the perfect whole person, body and soul working in perfect coordination. It is his body that will save ours, so often unruly and disobedient to the incorporeal faculties. Just as it is his animating principle alone that will sanctify ours, so it is to his body that we must turn when we are torn by temptation, racked by passion, weak in languor, dispirited with fatigue, when our bodily desires get out of hand. We cannot use ourselves as a psychological punching bag. We cannot order ourselves about with a: "Get in line there, body!" Rather, we need humbly to pray: "Body of Christ, save me!" I shall never save myself. This beautiful body of mine, this creation of God, can become the enemy of salvation just as my incorporeal faculties can. But the body of Christ can save me. Ought this not be a favorite prayer in time of temptation, of languor, of frustration, of sensual attraction, of sloth: "Body of Christ, save me!"

It is possible that the body can truly be all that it is destined to be in the mind of the Eternal Father, that it can achieve even here on earth some of the glory it will know fully only in heaven, but solely through the body of Christ. We look at his crucified body, and we can pray: "*Corpus Christi, salva me.*" He will, if allowed. He will save us if we know that we need salvation and cry out for it. We can allow our bodies their beautiful fulfillment in God's plan through a frequent turning to Christ in the Blessed Sacrament, but also through daily reflection on Christ's human nature as we see it in the Gospels. We shall be saved and shall be saving agents to one another, not of ourselves, but of Christ who truly dwells within us bodily at Holy

Communion, who presents himself to us throughout the Scriptures, but who is also present in all those around us as the Incarnate Word of God, the firstborn of all creation.

III

SANGUIS CHRISTI, INEBRIA ME

Blood of Christ, inebriate me

A$_{\text{ND SO WE COME TO THE THIRD PHRASE}}$ of the prayer *Anima Christi*. After having called out to the soul of Christ to sanctify us, having looked to his sacred body to save us from any misdirecting or misrepresenting of the role of our own body, we now plead: "*Sanguis Christi, inebria me*", "Blood of Christ, inebriate me", or, if you prefer your prayer more unabashedly literal: "Blood of Christ, make me drunk."

Unfortunately, we have come to associate with inebriation only one particular effect of a specific indulgence. We understand the literal kind of alcoholic drunkenness. Oh, but there is more to it than that! The kind of drunkenness we understand in our ordinary use of the word is a debasement of what true inebriation should be, that of which the poets and mystics have written when they said that they were drunk with the love of Christ, inebriated with God, set reeling with the thought of God's glory and of God's love for them.

In this prayer we return the word and the concept to truth. Although its ordinary use may represent a universally accepted meaning, still, beyond and beneath that is the stunning purity of the word and of the concept. Inebriation describes a state of exaltation, of enlivenment above what is ordinarily possible. And there immediately we come up against the intriguing consideration of how the present debased and almost sole use of the word, outside of mystical treatises or poetry, nevertheless preserves the lineaments of the actual and radical meaning. Do not many persons seek by the stimulation of alcohol, as many others also presently do by the use of drugs, to bring themselves to a state of enlivenment and of exhilaration beyond what they can otherwise achieve? Of course, because alcohol, actually a depressant, is only an artificial "stimulant" and drugs can be a really perverse stimulant; both overreach themselves as all artificialities and perversions must invariably do. The drunken person, that is, the alcoholic, may experience an initial exhilaration; but this quickly lapses into languor, stupor, and sometimes total unconsciousness. Drugs may have the same effect: initial exhilaration and enlivenment, and then the subsequent lassitude and final loss of consciousness.

With the inebriation of the spirit, it is different.

Here are the true exhilaration and enlivenment that lift us above and beyond the ordinary in truth and purity. And this is what the Church proposes to us in this prayer: that we should be enlivened, lifted up above our ordinary functioning, abilities, even potential, by the precious blood of Christ. It is in this sense that the saints and the mystics have so well understood it. Certainly it was a mystic who wrote this prayer.

"Blood of Christ, inebriate me!" A very bold prayer in a very accurate expression of a truth both stark and glorious. It is in this sense that the soul should be inebriated. Unlike the debasing inebriation that artificial stimuli produce, this inebriation is not of the senses. It may have nothing whatsoever to do with emotional response or lack of response. It means that the spirit is enlivened, and the body exhilarated, not by what they feel but by what they can do. We see something of this in the Acts of the Apostles when, on the first Pentecost morning, the disciples were speaking with such enlivenment as no one had seen in them before. They were addressing the crowds with an exhilaration that was completely new and far beyond their own powers and ordinary way of acting. The Pentecostal apostles were obviously exceeding their own potential. So the people concluded they were drunk: "They are filled with new wine!" (Acts 2:13). Well, they were, in a more profound sense than those listening to and accusing them could ever have dreamed. They were inebriated with the blood of Christ, whose effects the Holy Spirit was at that moment bringing to climactic action. And whenever we are enabled by the Holy Spirit to exceed ourselves, to surpass our natural capabilities, we are experiencing in our measure and expressing within our possibilities the inebriation that is the effect of the blood of Christ outpoured.

It is the spilled blood of Christ that through the ages has inebriated souls to the point of martyrdom. One has to be enlivened beyond one's own possibilities to be a martyr. One has to be, in the mystical and profoundly spiritual sense, quite drunk—with God. The martyrs were the outstanding inebriates, enlivened and exhilarated beyond their nature, their potential. Nature clings fiercely to life. The spiritual inebriate runs singing to martyrdom. All the saints of God were inebriated by the blood of Christ. And if we are to excel our own meager possibilities, we must also be made drunk with that most precious blood. It is the blood of Christ alone that can enliven us to respond with a service beyond ourselves, that can achieve the overextension of ourselves without harm and, in fact, with glory. It is a glorious outcry, this *"Sanguis Christi, inebria me!"* We need so much to be lifted above ourselves and beyond ourselves into God in order that, thus situated, we can become most truly ourselves. Just as we considered earlier on in this prayer that we are most fully ourselves when we have that mind in us which was also in Christ Jesus (Phil 2:5), so are we best using, even best understanding, our own bodies when we see ourselves saved by the body of Christ. We are enabled to do the impossible when we are inebriated with the blood of Christ.

In considering the unfortunate usual meaning of inebriation, we see a certain parallel there in that first exhilaration and false enlivenment of which we spoke before. There follows the stupor, the spirit's inevitable comment on artificiality. In much the same way, when we simulate a storm of emotion or a hurricane of passion, we can be made somehow to experience a strength beyond ourselves for a brief moment. But because it is artificial or perverse or both, it quickly degenerates into the precisely opposite effect. It is easy to see, though, in those first stages, a fleeting strength beyond the ordinary. Scientists and doctors have observed often enough how a drunken person can weave his way along, avoiding danger, with a sureness beyond himself. Again, a person in the first stages of drunkenness can often evince a strength he does not appear to have when sober, as he staggers unharmed through all manner of life-threatening dangers of traffic, heights, descents. In the true inebriation of the spirit, the antithesis of all that is perverse or evil or self-indulgent, there is a strength beyond what we could ever have of ourselves but which never lapses into languor. It is always turned outward, never inward. Spiritual inebriation is borne witness to, not by what I feel, but by what I do.

If the martyrs often enough went singing and jesting to martyrdom, it was because they were inebriated with Christ, strong beyond themselves. For the body does not wish to die. We have reflected already on how the body comments in the tomb on its temporary separation from the soul in a chilling way that is permitted and even penitentially imposed by God. But for the body to desire death in the loftiness of martyrdom, not as an escape, not as the manic depressive might desire death, but in the flaming love of Christ that knows that if to live is Christ, "to die is gain" (Phil 1:21), it needs the inebriating effects of the blood of Christ.

When the martyrs went smiling and singing to martyrdom, it was because they were drunk with the blood of Christ. And when we go singing, not necessarily emotionally, but with that great *desiderium* of the will, which functions with or without the supportive factor of emotion, into daily little dyings, it is again the effect of the blood of Christ. In all the hidden, humdrum martyrdoms that are part of real Christian daily living, one must be inebriated to agree to them singing. In all the little sacrifices of each day when God cheerfully invites us: "Come, and die!" we can respond with a joy more profound than a merely human one. One needs only to have an inebriated heart, able to transcend its natural limitations and to follow a difficult path with unstumbling feet. "Yes! I will die." We die to our own preferences; we die to the tart response that nature quickly frames when we are offended; we die to the caustic reply that pride proposes; we die to the sensual urges that often surprise us with their insistence. One goes singing into all these invitations to the little deaths of every day only when one is inebriated with the blood of Christ.

In the lives of Saint Francis of Assisi and Saint Clare, we certainly observe this inebriation. Saint Francis was so drunk with the love of God, so inebriated with the blood of Christ, that he spent his whole life excelling himself and exceeding his own possibilities. Saint Clare was another true inebriate of the blood of Christ, surpassing her own human possibilities throughout her whole life, in the stand she unflinchingly took and maintained, in the faith that never wavered, in her long and arduous illness, in the disappointments and frustrations and faith-testings that were her ordinary fare. She surpassed herself and raised up in the Church of God a great Order, its like before unknown, because she was inebriated with the blood of Christ.

This inebriation is there for us also. Why can we not make it our prayer, our faith? When what is asked of us in daily life seems to our niggardliness and fear to be just too much, too much to give, too much patience to sustain, too much meekness to achieve, it remains wholly possible to turn to Christ, who shed all his precious blood that we might be inebriated by its effects, to achieve ends far beyond our own unaided powers. Why not turn to what is so accessible to us in the merits of the precious blood of Christ and become inebriated with it, so that we might have a strength that can discover: "No, that is not too much! I can do it. I can lift the weight of this cross. I can sustain this activity. I can suffer this oppression. I am inebriated! I have a strength beyond the ordinary. And all because I am possessed of the inebriating power that arises out of union with Christ."

Could this not be a precious aspiration of our daily life on all the occasions that seem "too much"? Could we not turn to Christ, look at him upon that Cross, and say: "Agreed. It is too much for me as I am. I would need a strength beyond my own. And that strength awaits my begging: 'Blood of Christ, inebriate me!'"

The merits of Christ have been given to us, delivered over to us by the Father through the Passion and death of his divine Son, and they are quite sufficient to make of us true spiritual inebriates. The more that some things seem "too much", the more inebriation we need. And so the more we must turn to the precious blood of Christ streaming out through all his sacraments, given to us every morning in Holy Communion, cleansing us in every sacramental absolution, and also mysteriously washing over us in every actual grace as well as every increase of sanctifying grace. Why leave untapped the resources we have to be spiritual inebriates to whom no sacrifice at all is too much? *"Sanguis Christi, inebria nos!"*

IV

AQUA LATERIS CHRISTI, LAVA ME

Water from the side of Christ, wash me

WE MIGHT PERHAPS CALL the next petition the most mystical of them all. We pray, "*Aqua lateris Christi, lava me*", "Water from the side of Christ, wash me." There is a very intimate connection between the blood that was shed and that water from Christ's side. At a recent assembly, my sisters and I were musing together on the beauty of the altar décor, reflecting on the theme in Holy Scripture that "out of his heart shall flow rivers of living water" (Jn 7:38). And indeed it was a most charming décor, with light gauze cloth signifying the flowing water, and the "water" caught below in a pure white bowl with its floating mimosa blossoms amid ornamental rocks. A true presentation. Mystics through the centuries have made such presentations in their words, their songs, their dance, whatever creative outlets they chose for sharing with us their understanding of what was flowing from the side of Christ. But these lovely mystical representations, like any true mystical representation, express a very solid reality, a reality so overwhelmingly strong that it can perhaps only be rightly expressed in mystical form.

What, really, was that water that came from the side of Christ, after all the bitter sufferings, the agony of the scourging, the crowning with thorns, the painful and arduous way of the Cross, the anguished affixing to the Cross, the three terrible hours of agony of body and soul and mind and heart? What was this that happened after all the rest was done and Jesus had said, "It is finished" (Jn 19:30)? What took place after his "Father, into your hands I commit my spirit" (Lk 23:46) was spoken, and his spirit, committed, had indeed gone into the hands of his Father? What was this flow of water from his side?

We know that the human heart is enclosed in a conical sac of liquid and that the sac is called the pericardium. This serous membrane which surrounds the heart is, in a sense, the heart's last protection. When that soldier took that spear and plunged it into the side of Christ, he pierced the pericardium of the God-Man. Along with the last drop of blood of that Sacred Heart came its support, that clear liquid from the pericardium. The definitive sign of death.

The support was gone, the pericardium pierced, and water flowing to proclaim death reiterated in its own way the proclamation that his blessed lips had uttered only a few moments before: "It is finished." There is nothing more to give. The name of the water from the side of Christ is: totality. The sheltering sac around the heart has been pierced and the heart itself rent. The water and the blood now announce together: "All is given."

When the Scriptures tell us "out of his heart shall flow rivers of living water" (Jn 7:38), they are asking us to remember that the living water we received from the sacred side is the water proclaiming Christ's death but is likewise living water for us, the baptizing of the new Church born from that side of his. Strength is always received from one who gives all.

In every reference to this water from the side of Christ we see, in the Scriptures as well as in the writings of the mystics through the centuries, the expression of totality. In the first Vespers hymn of the Solemnity of the most Sacred Heart of Jesus, we have these words: "For this you bore the lance's thrust and scourge and thorns and pains,/ that blood and water from your Heart might wash away our stains." And all that led up to this emphasizes that everything Christ bore was ordered toward this totality of giving, the flowing of water and blood from his stricken side.

Again, in one of the responsories in the Office of the most Sacred Heart, we have these words: "Christ has loved us, and in his blood he has washed away our sins." But also, in the intercessions, "Jesus, whose heart when pierced . . . poured forth blood and water and gave birth to . . . the Church." Was the blood not enough, his lifeblood that gave life to the Church? Indeed it was. But the water from his side is the most dramatic sign of all. The Church is born from his sacred side, out of his total giving. And we are born, baptized, and saved out of his total giving, without which neither birth nor baptism nor salvation could be possible. It is the sign of his death which is the sign of our life.

As sons and daughters of the Church, we have a specific delegated mission: to wash away the sins of the world and to send out streams of living waters upon a continually dying, agonizing, anguished world. We cannot do this unless our own spiritual pericardium is broken and all is given, so that from us, too, in union with his infinite giving, flow out blood and water, the sign of death. We shall give life to no one except at the cost of some dying of ours. For no one ever gives new life, renewed life, a new reason to live, a stout will to live, nor is anyone ever a channel of eternal life, except at the cost of some personal dying. If the Church was born from the side of Christ at that moment when blood and the water flowed forth in a sign of totality, and if we were indeed cleansed from our stains in that moment and in that sign of his total giving, and if we draw strength from that stream of water which is living water for us because it is the water of death for him, it shall never be otherwise with our own giving.

If we do not wish to die, we cannot delude ourselves into thinking that we can be purveyors of life. And if we are not willing for our spiritual pericardia to be pierced and torn in labor, fatigue, suffering, misunderstanding, or frustration by whatever lances or cudgels may be, we cannot be what Jesus wants us to be: finite channels of living water out of our many daily dyings.

We read in Romans, "For your sake we are being killed all the day long" (8:36). This is an expression that any lover would be able to understand. When we love totally, it is a happy thing to be slain for the beloved. Do we not see this in all profound human love? A mother would rejoice to give her life for her child. A very terrible marginal note on our own times tells of mothers who destroy the lives of their children and thus pervert the whole concept and reality of motherhood. It is of the essence of motherhood that the mother would gladly die for her child. Nature herself will rise up in revenge on the mother content to have her child die that she might live as she chooses. Love always seeks to give at its own expense and at the sacrifice of itself.

Have we not all experienced something of this?

The joy of being worn out in doing something for one we love? The joy of exhaustion in serving those we esteem? Far from its being masochistic that we should find happiness in dying that we might give, this lies at the healthy and happy heart of love itself. Sometimes we witness this rather dramatically in ourselves. We are conscious of being tempted, not to give, but rather to sit down and enjoy our self-pity, fatigue, disappointment, or hurt. Then, by God's grace, we make a great effort to rise out of that and to die to it. And we experience deep spiritual joy. We decide, not to live in self-pity or disappointment or hurt, but to die to them so that we might give, through Christ, understanding or strength or new clarity of mind to another. And, behold, we rise! There are many ways to die in order that others might live. We shall understand much more about this in eternity, but we can experience it on earth, in time.

The Scriptures tell us again that in Jesus "is the fountain of life" (Ps 36:9), and the Office of the most Sacred Heart tells us in another antiphon that "we drink from the streams of [his] goodness". We drink from the streams of death flowing from his side. And we live. The stream that flows out from us, too, upon the world cannot be a death-giving stream of self-involvement, a bitter stream of acrimony or aggressiveness, a turgid stream of self-pity and selfishness and sloth, but a life-giving stream of goodness.

Goodness, the philosophers tell us, is diffusive of itself. And Jesus has implanted his goodness in us. We are made in the image of God and, thus, in the image of goodness. That goodness, however, has been bruised and hurt by original sin. It has been enfeebled by our many actual sins. But by total giving, our faltering goodness is reunited with the goodness of the Father and flows out in streams of living water. It ought to be possible for the world to say of any true Christian that same antiphon: "We drink from the streams of your goodness." How could we offer poisoned waters, tainted waters, turgid waters to a world that has a right to come to us and say: "All right, as Christians you are there to live a penitential life of prayer and of dying. We have come to drink the living water that flows from your dying." For, yes, the world has a right to come and to receive.

Water is so beautiful. No wonder Saint Francis sang of it with particular tenderness in his Canticle of the Creatures. "Be praised, my Lord, for our sister water. So great is she and yet remains so humble, shining in her crystal chastity." There is a clear, a shining water in the pericardium, the supporting sac of the heart. And it was a beautiful sister water indeed that flowed from the side of Christ as the sign of his death, clear water from his human pericardium and mystical water from his Godhead. The water of dying is always clear, always life-giving. It is the water of selfishness that is

44

tainted, discolored, disease-bringing. If we want to bring life to the world, life to the Church, we shall do this only as Jesus did it: by dying. The clear water that flows from each little human dying can be made by Christ a new stream of living water.

Returning to that familiar quotation from Romans, "for your sake we are being killed all the day long", we remember that this is not a groan, a lament, a jeremiad. It is a proclamation. It is like the clear water from the pierced pericardium, the water of total giving, it is a cry of joy! "For *your* sake we are being killed all the day long." The little dyings God allows us in our lives *are* for his sake; they are not for no reason. The sacrifices to which Christ's graces and inspirations invite us, to which the needs of others summon us, to which the anguish of the world beckons us are not meaningless dyings, not bitter things. The apostle Saint Paul was not muttering or groaning when he said that we are killed all the day long. No, he was making a joyous proclamation. "It's wonderful!" is what he was saying. Which was by no means to say that his human body was dancing for joy, but only that his spirit was.

And so it was when the water came from the side of Christ, flowing out as a sign of his total giving. All was given, all was over, the dying complete. And we were saved. All of this we confess when we pray, "Water from the side of Christ, wash me." It has cleansing, laving powers because it is the sign of totality, pouring out at the lance-thrust that tells his death. We are washed by that water, the Church is born of that water and baptized in that water because it is the water of consummation. The sign of his death is the sign of our life. And in the same manner, if not degree, we shall wash one another to new life only out of our willing dyings.

In all of our lives there come times when we think we cannot do anything about some untoward situation or that we cannot help some particular person. We feel that we have exhausted all our efforts, even all our hopes. Everything seems in vain. But this is never so. It is only that we have not died enough deaths or not died totally in this situation or for this person. For her son, Augustine, Monica died on and on and on. And Saint Augustine was washed into a new life by the total giving of Christ flowing out upon him through Saint Monica's dying.

It is a beautiful mystical reflection, that from Christ's side flow streams of living water, but we need to remember that it is the stream of his dying that is our living water. When we pray, "*Aqua lateris Christi, lava me*", it is not a true prayer unless we are including in it the desire for our own dying out of Christ's dying. It must be a sincere prayer that our spiritual pericardia may be pierced and we ourselves left without support or mainstay save in God, so that others may live. It is a very bold prayer, a very dangerous prayer. It is a petition that we may be given the strength ourselves to die totally so that others may live.

V

PASSIO CHRISTI, CONFORTA ME

Passion of Christ, comfort me

Advancing along the consecutive petitions in the time-honored prayer *Anima Christi*, we arrive at the one of which all the others are part. We pray: "*Passio Christi, conforta me*", "Passion of Christ, comfort me." Comfort me—yes; but in the very literal and etymological sense of that word: make me strong. Passion of Christ, make me strong.

Surely that is a prayer we should like to make our own, for we would rejoice to be strong in our sufferings from the strength of the Passion of Christ. But this does not always seem to happen. In fact, we see all too manifestly that it often enough does not occur. We seem, instead, very weak. Where is that strength from the Passion of Christ? Perhaps we need to recall that it is not effected *ex opere operato*. Our Lord suffered, endured, willingly accepted his Passion and death; therefore, we are strong. Strength flows out of him to us indeed, but not without our effort to receive it. Three considerations present themselves about making effective the strength that is there for us in the Passion of Christ. The first is that it is necessary for us to remember the Passion of Christ, to focus upon it. The second is that it is required that we identify with the Passion of Christ. And the third consideration is that we must accept responsibility for the strength with which the Passion of Christ empowers us.

So now, the initial consideration. We need to remember. At first blush, we might avow that the Passion of Christ is something we certainly never forget. Yet, in fact, we know that we forget it quite easily. We forget it in the way we tend to forget all things that are familiar to us. We have seen the crucifix all our lives. It is so familiar that we can all too readily forget what it means. It takes effort to remember, to focus. We see this exemplified in other areas of our life with regard to the dear familiars. We could recall, for instance, how we know and cherish all that our forebears did for us, all that they suffered, all their labors as they strove to provide for our welfare and our future. But to remember this effectively when we have some hardship set before us, to focus upon this when something difficult is asked of us—ah, that is a different matter. An example of remembering comes vividly and poignantly to mind: Dismas, the good thief.

We go back in time two thousand years, and we

find this thief whom tradition has immortalized as "Saint Dismas, the good thief". That calls for a short intermission for smiling. What is a good thief? One efficient in his work, alert for opportunities for thieving, admirably clever in performance? Admittedly, "Dismas, the thief who gave up thieving for goodness" is rather a mouthful. But we ought at least in our silent understanding to recall that Saint Dismas was awarded Paradise, right then and there, the same day, because he went to confession there on his cross and made one of the most stirring general confessions in history, which is to say: no excuse, no shifting of responsibility, no censure laid on his parents, upbringing, or bad companions at an early age. He came without excuse but just with a wonderfully profound act of faith, enlightened enough to know that the dying Jesus was divinely equipped to sort out Dismas' past record and was assuredly marveling at Dismas' faith illumined by the Holy Spirit. We see him there on his cross, sharing the ignominious death of our Lord and asking Jesus to remember him. Those words of his shake our hearts with their grandeur, "Lord, remember me when you come into your kingdom" (Lk 23:42). However, before Dismas could make that prayer to be remembered, he had himself first to remember.

Dismas was hearing some strange words from this Person on that center Cross, and he was seeing some very unusual features of this Person there dying. The thief on the third cross heard the same words, saw the same phenomena. Tradition has called him "the bad thief". Certainly he made a bad choice. He chose not to remember. This man, too, heard words such as undoubtedly he had never heard before, things that went far, far beyond the possibility of mere human nobility. He heard that dying Person on the center Cross say, for instance, "Father, forgive them; for they know not what they do" (Lk 23:34). And then he forgot what he had heard. The dying Christ was not only uttering the immortal plea for mercy on one's persecutors that saints and martyrs have echoed all the centuries after him, but he was also really proclaiming his divinity. He was turning to his Father with assurance and telling the Father what to do as only an equal could.

The martyrs who through the ages have uttered forgiving words like those of Jesus could not speak them as he did. Christ could say, "They know not know what they do", for he really did know what they knew. He knew who he was and that they did not. He had no such plea for Caiaphas because Caiaphas did know. And so to Caiaphas, Jesus only replied: "You say that I am" (Lk 22:70). What a different course Caiaphas would have taken if he had chosen to remember the truth he heard instead of theatrically and deceitfully rending his garments. And there is Pilate, poor craven Pilate, not with Caiaphas' knowledge, but with a fearsome glimmer of the truth. "Upon this Pilate sought to release him" (Jn 19:12). But Pilate succumbed to his fear of the mob and fear for his paltry position, choosing not to remember what had struck his soul. Dismas, though, heard and remembered.

Dismas heard the grandeur with which the dying man delivered his mother over as a heritage to his beloved disciple, heard the agonizing Person on the center Cross giving clear directions about what was to be done and identifying the roles of other persons. This is your son now, go with him. This is your mother; take her. Father, forgive these people. And Dismas did not turn back upon himself as did the other thief, nor did he cry out as his companion did, and as so many others have done in the extreme of human agony, in vituperative rage at those who suffer nobly and well, as though that were the final outrage. The other thief turned in upon himself, forgot what he saw, forgot what he heard, and so jeered at our Lord. Dismas remembered and gave his own marvelous cry for remembrance.

So it is with us. We can only truly pray, "Passion of Christ, make me strong", when we have started remembering the Passion of Christ. It is not a magic formula, this prayer. I utter it, and something happens. It is more than a little amazing when well-intentioned "devotional writers" say something to the effect that just this little statement of Dismas gained him Paradise. Little statement? It was a tremendous response. Dismas allowed God to lift him out of himself into the realms of pure faith. He begins his response to remembering by saying, "Lord!" No one who had not been lifted by God into the realm of faith could possibly have said this. Christ just did not much look like "Lord" then. The messianic psalms come crowding in upon us: "The LORD said to my Lord . . ." (Ps 110:1). The grandeur! But this bruised, bleeding, spent, helpless Person—to recognize him as "Lord"! This is magnificent. Dismas does not say, "Sir" or "Friend", or "We are in this together." "Lord!" "Lord, remember me." And Jesus knew that Dismas had remembered him. "Remember me when you come into your kingdom" (Lk 23:42). With that plea Dismas reached the heights of mysticism. Could it look to any other's gaze that this battered Person had a kingdom? That he even belonged to a kingdom? That he could make his way into a kingdom? But Dismas is saying: "It's all yours! It is your kingdom. And when you take over your kingdom, remember me."

Through all the centuries we have had a plethora of exquisite poetry and a plenitude of mystical effusions from chosen souls of whom Dismas was the prototype. All the glorious poetry about Christ robed in the royal robes of his blood, Christ triumphant upon the Cross—was not Dismas the first one to say all these things? Dismas spoke of royalty. He is the

53

prototype of all Christian poets of the Cross. His is the first mystical vision of what was happening on the Cross. This is a King. This is the Lord. He is in royal splendor; and when he comes to take over his kingdom, I hope to be remembered. So we, too, have to remember in everyday life. To remember when it is difficult to remember. Dismas could have remembered only his own misery, as did his fellow thief, and he could have sunk to the same despairing depths. Instead he allowed the strength of what he remembered to let him become, among other things, the poet laureate of all those who have sung of the Royal One dying upon the Cross.

Yes, there must be the remembering of the Passion of Christ, a focusing upon it. But we also have to identify with it. We can often enough find homely examples of that in our own lives. When we made a foundation in Virginia, there was so much to be done in converting the little convent loaned to us into a temporary monastery. We needed to revamp the place, to convert it into a monastic dwelling. And we needed to do this in the brief two weeks I had with our founding sisters. So, we moved very fast to many corners in a strange dwelling. Inevitably there were many bumps and jars. I remember bumping an arm here, a leg there, something hurting where I had overstretched in reaching. But we were too eagerly busy to stop to investigate the battle scars. It was only when I returned home to Roswell that I really had time to notice that my limbs were covered with bruises. There they were: bruises and bruises, on my arms, on my lower limbs. And one most marvelous bruise! I think it was about four inches long and three inches wide, and in colors gorgeous to behold.

There was joy in seeing those bruises. They reminded me of all I had wanted to do for our sisters, of all that we had done together. They were such beautiful little emblems of our earnest desire to do something beautiful for God. When the last bruise began to fade, I felt a little sadness at seeing it disappear, so glad was I to have been bruised in trying to work with and help sisters so dearly loved. Easily the reflection opens out that we can never help one another spiritually, either, if we do not wish to be bruised. With an unbruised heart we shall never love.

Indeed, it is inevitable that when we really love, we shall get bruised. While we are often reminded that our Lord has his glorified wounds in heaven and that he shows them to the Father as pleading on our behalf ("*Ostende vulnera tua ad Patrem*", we beseech him), it is a matter not only of offering those wounds on our behalf but also—let us dare to say it—our Lord rejoicing in his own glorified wounds. This is not fantasy, for do we not have the Scriptures telling us, "Was it not ordained that the Christ should suffer and *so* enter into his glory?" (Lk 24:26; emphasis added). It is as though Christ brushes aside all of his Passion and says, "Oh, a mere nothing! I love these people. I wanted to save them. It was nothing at all. Was it not ordained that the Christ should have suffered this . . ." Well, then, does he not rejoice in his glorified wounds? Are they not a continual "reminder" to him, those emblems, of how much he loved and does love us? It is part of Franciscan Scotist theology that Christ came, not only because of our need as a fallen race to be redeemed, but as the firstborn of all creation to teach us how to live. One cannot teach life except by getting a wounded heart, a wounded spirit, not without being bruised.

We see the parable of the bruises readily enough on the physical plane. Surely no one would say: "Look at all the bruises I got helping those people. Someone had the nerve!" No, one is just so happy to have served and to have mementos of the service. It is not quite so obvious to us on the emotional level and still less on the spiritual plane, the understanding of those bruises upon the skin of the heart and the spirit. We must study to learn how to identify also the bruises of the heart and the spirit with the Passion of Christ, who did not love us without getting bruised in the process. We have those soul-shaking lines from Holy Scripture, almost too exquisitely acute to bear: "With his stripes we are healed" (Is 53:5). His wounds have not healed us of our need of being wounded but of the

wound of our self-centeredness. His wounds have
called us to come out of self, to be made strong in
suffering. This is to identify with the Passion of Christ.

The third and final consideration, then, is the responsibility that the Passion of Christ enjoins upon
us. We dare not underestimate the strength we have
once we have been redeemed in love by Jesus. When
we make promises to God, we cannot disavow the
power put into us to observe them faithfully. When
we are given by God any circumstance, any work to
do, any suffering to sustain, we are also given the
power and the strength to do or to suffer it. So, when
remembering and focusing in our identification with
the Passion of Christ, we need also to make active his
own mandate through the inspired word of his apostle,
that "in my flesh I complete what is lacking in Christ's
afflictions" (Col 1:24). What is lacking in Christ's Passion in me? It is my own bruises of body, of heart, of
spirit, bruises of disappointment, bruises of frustration, bruises of misunderstanding, bruises of ingratitude, bruises perhaps of rejection. Aware of this,
remembering, focused, identified, we can truly pray,
"Passion of Christ, make me strong!" We dare not
pray it unless we are prepared to accept the responsibility of having the strength of the Passion of Jesus
given to us.

When Dismas made his petition and his exalted act
of faith and homage, does not the very instinct for

truth tell us that Christ responded as God, that his dying head lifted? How could he have replied as he did with his beautiful, suffering, bloody, battered head sunk upon his chest? We know that he answered as a King. He used royal words and began his statement as he began all his other statements of great authority and solemnity: "Amen, I say to you." A king is speaking. "This day." Authority. There is no doubt about it. He knows the time and the hour. "Today you will be with me in Paradise" (Lk 23:43). After that, the dying head doubtless drooped again. But Dismas had received the strength that was given; and even as we must, he had to accept the responsibility for what he had been given.

We know how Saint Paul loved to enumerate all the things he had done and suffered for Christ. Certainly he is not boasting: Look at Paul—what a great fellow he is! No, he is marveling at what Christ's Passion did in him when he allowed it. In this way he says: I was flogged this many times, I was shipwrecked, I endured this, I suffered that—a whole list of things (2 Cor 11:24ff.). But this is the same man who said: Take this temptation away; it's too much. We know that Christ said: No. Be strong in infirmity. "My grace is sufficient for you" (2 Cor 12:9). And Saint Paul let himself be made strong in infirmity. That is why he can later say: "Listen to this!"

All of us can look back on our own little lives and

search out instances in which we have allowed God to let us surpass ourselves. Because we are redeemed by Christ's obedience in his Passion and death, we no longer have the right to say: I cannot do it. Strength has been given. So now we pray: "Passion of Christ, make me strong", knowing that first of all we must remember it, then focus upon it, then identify our own bruises as making up in us what is wanting in his Passion. We begin to join our own hesitant refrain to his great theme: "Was it not necessary that I suffer this?" Was it not ordained that I should suffer for all the world? Was it not ordained that I suffer for the benefactors who befriend us and for those others who think our life a waste? "Passion of Christ, make me strong." Yes, it is a dangerous prayer. For if I ask to be made strong in this way, I *will* be made strong and have to abdicate any further right to say, "I can't." In this prayer I deliver up to Christ my former right to say, "I cannot do it."

VI

O BONE JESU, EXAUDI ME

O good Jesus, hear me

WE MOVE ALONG IN THE PRAYER *Anima Christi* to a very simple invocation that one might think is a kind of resting point in this daring prayer. We have called upon the soul of Christ to achieve something in us; we have turned to the body of Christ in a very particular way; we have asked to be made drunk by the blood of Christ and to be enabled to flow out in life through self-giving death by the power of the water from the side of Christ. We have begged to be made strong in the Passion of Christ. Is this particular place to which we have come in the prayer indicative of a time to sit down, relax, and serenely ask: "*O bone Jesu, exaudi me*", "O good Jesus, hear me"? No, it is not just a pause between the invocations and ardent petitions of a lover. Rather, we are rising to a climactic point where we look back upon what we have already asked in order to go forward to make even bolder prayers.

We cry out on this bridge of the prayer, "O good Jesus, hear me." A bridge spans waters. We are supposed to walk across a bridge. It is a place for action. On little rustic bridges over small streams, one may perhaps pause to dream and reflect. This is not that kind of bridge. It is a bridge to be immediately crossed over. A bridge is basically meant to be, not an end in itself, but a means of going toward something else, a method for arriving.

When we say, "O good Jesus, hear me", we want to be reminded of what we are asking, where we are daring to desire to go. Hearing increases with listening. We need to be reminded in our times more than once about the importance of listening; it has become in many areas a lost art. We know that often what we hear is not what the person means. We hear only words. Our need is to become adept at hearing to a point where we can listen to what is beneath the words, to what the person actually intends, which may or may not be fully known even to the person speaking.

There are ready examples from our common human condition. We have the bully. Sometimes there are bullies among children, sometimes there are bullies among adults. We have a lot of bullying in the "thinking" in our times among those who, at least chronologically speaking, have left childhood far behind. What we hear coming from the mouth of the

bully is the determination to dominate, to back someone to a wall, to look down at this person and oblige
him to do what the bully wishes. Thus his words be-
speak domination, aggressiveness. However, if we have
learned to listen beneath the words and actions of the
child-bully or the adult-bully, what we will hear is
something quite different from his words. We shall
hear about that person's fear and sense of inferiority,
because only the person who feels inferior has the
need to domineer. In this facile example, we see that
we cannot be convinced that we have listened just
because we have heard some words, or that we understand just because we have seen certain actions.

Again, there is the example of the coward. We often hear from the mouth of the coward a great deal of
boasting. If we have learned to listen to the coward,
beneath what our ears deliver to our brain, then we
hear about a fear of truth. The coward has to boast
because the truth seems beyond him. One of the great
army generals of modern times, Marshal Foch, I believe, said, "Any soldier who tells me that he has never
been afraid in battle either has never been in a battle
or is a liar." The truth to be admitted is that in battle
one's normal and healthy response is to be afraid. A
brave person does not hesitate to confront this healthy
truth and to say: "I am afraid." The coward has not
reached this liberation of truth; and so we often hear
from him boasting, sometimes sheer fabrication. How-

ever, if we listen in love, we may hear a plea to be liberated into the truth, into an ability to face and express the truth.

Likewise, there is the slothful person who often enough (or more often than enough) speaks with insolence. At least this is what our ears hear from the slothful person. But what the ears of a listening heart hear from a slothful person is the fear of being recruited to generosity. One encounters insolent casualness. Under that, to the listening heart, is the fluttering fear of being captured to do something that costs, a fear of being recruited into a liberation of self, a responsibility that person is not willing to accept and which he must be helped by love to face.

Finally, there is the insecure person who batters our ears with excuses, sometimes even with fantastic fabrications, who can cross the line into sheer prevarication. What the loving heart that listens hears beneath this flood of excuses and manipulations of reality is the pathetic little cry of the one who feels he has no margin for error. The secure person has a very wide margin for errors, knows that he will make many mistakes in life and is able to confess them with mature good humor born of healthy humility. He is liberated into the truth, and so we do not hear those little bleating cries of weakness.

In any of these examples—the coward, the bully, the slothful, the insecure—what we hear is often the opposite of the truth. Our ears hear on an upper and often superficial level; the listening heart hears something very different and sometimes even opposite. The bully is the one who feels inferior; the coward is the one afraid of the truth; the slothful is the person with a fear of being led into generosity; the insecure is the person with no margin for error. We want to be good listeners, going beneath the surface of mere hearing.

In the prayer *Anima Christi* we ask Jesus to hear us. What we really ask him to do is to listen to what we dare not articulate, what maybe we ourselves do not even understand at this point in our lives. Our aching intent is to say, "You are a good Jesus. When you hear, you listen." Returning to our four examples, what would we do if we were really listening to the interior cry of these persons? What response would we then make? It would surely be quite different from the response of merely hearing, which, for example, would want to super-dominate the domineering bully, whereas the listening heart would desire with love to establish the bully in his own personhood, rooted in Jesus, whose Personhood is God. Having helped to establish a person in his own radiant personhood, we have helped him discover that he has no need to domineer.

If we are really listening to the cowardly person instead of just hearing the embarrassing boasting, we would be able to respond with understanding so that he could be helped to arrive at a normal response. If we are really listening, not just hearing words and being annoyed and disaffected by the slothful person, we could help to establish for him a goal of givenness, not by preaching, but by showing forth in our own lives that we have a goal of givenness and that we are always striving, if not always successfully, to achieve it and that we find the striving itself already rewarding. If we listen, instead of just hearing the facile fabrications and excuses of the insecure, then by our own faith in Jesus we can show the one of interior knocking knees that he really can, just as everyone can, do all things in him who strengthens us (cf. Phil 4:13). We teach—not so much in words or homiletics as by our own way of living—that a person really can do all that he is asked. And can afford to say that he is wrong when he fails.

A superior certainly must learn to listen to the cry of her spiritual daughter, for it may be the exact opposite of what the person is saying. When the aggressive person spouts her aggressiveness, the superior must not stop at hearing this eruption of psychological lava, but she must rather listen to the crying need for disciplining that aggressiveness into the beautiful strength and leadership that it was designed by God to be. She has to listen and to teach that truth does not destroy but makes us free. She has to listen in the way the saints listened and were able to say, like Saint Philip

Neri, "Hold me by the hand today, Lord, or I shall surely betray you." She has to help the one who tends to be cowardly to know that this is what we all must face: fear. Saint Francis was never more chaste than when he said, "Pray for me, for I may yet have children." She must listen to the true need and help the other achieve the truth, responding to the real need in one who is slothful and ungenerous, which is to become able to feel a need greater than her own, and helping her rejoice to be driven by a love that is so much more impelling than the love of her own convenience, her own designs, her own selfish purposes.

If a superior—or anyone else, for that matter—hears only words, she can easily become very discouraged. If, however, she listens to the little wordless crying need that says: "I do not know yet what it is to experience needs greater than my own. Will you help me?" she will be urged to respond on a more profound level to a deeper need. With the insecure she will strive to make the person greater than her weakness by bringing her to an ability to acknowledge her weakness and infidelity. She must listen especially to that person's great longing to be assured that she is still loved when her weakness, her infidelity, her failures have high visibility. For there is that wonderful security of realizing that others see our weakness and failures and so, in loving us, are not loving a phantasm or illusion but the real person—the stumbler, fumbler, babbler, sinner. Yes, that is a wonderful thing! Above all, to remember that God holds the complete folio of our miseries and still loves us and that he, this good Jesus, listens to something beneath what we are saying, hearing the real cry of the heart even when we do not hear it ourselves.

We have to love enough to be able to listen to real needs. So, in the inevitable little "situations" of life that must occur where real human beings live an authentic life together, we can learn to hear beneath an impatient word the need to be disciplined and respond to what the listening heart has heard, not just to what our ears have delivered to the brain. Listening, we learn to respond, sometimes with a smile, sometimes with humor, sometimes with an expression of disappointment. How shall we know which is the proper response? Only by being persons of prayer. When we are persons of prayer, it will be given us in that hour what to say and what not to say, what to do and what not to do. We shall know how to listen so that we may understand how to reply. Our listening will have gone far beneath hearing. We will be good hearers like Jesus, which means to be a listener.

When we pray: "O good Jesus, hear me!" the soul is really crying out: "Jesus, only my *words* are saying that I need to be pitied, coddled; I've had a hard time and I need to be soothed." We are making another dangerous prayer. For we are saying: "O *good* Jesus", and because he is so good, he responds, not to the articulated need, but to the real one. He does not just hear, he listens. To our expressed need to be soothed and coddled, he responds with the occasion for greater sacrifice.

We all laughed a little when we read in recent notes from our sisters at our new foundation: "We have our straw mattresses now, and already there is a great improvement in muscle tone!" This is how our good Jesus answers us. We are saying in one way or another: "I am tired. I need a spiritual innerspring mattress." Jesus, however, knows the need for muscle tone, and he gives us a hard spiritual bed to lie on. He listens deeply because he loves us deeply, because he is our *good* Jesus. Being good, he often cannot give what our words are asking. He listens to the spirit, and he always responds. When our words, articulated aloud or spoken only in the chamber of the mind, complain: "I am misunderstood", Jesus listens and replies, "I understand you perfectly. And I still love you. You have no need to play-act." Our words cry out to him, "O Jesus, I cannot do it." But we are talking to a good Jesus, who listens to the true need of the soul created by the Father in his own image and partaking through him of his omnipotence, so that we can do whatever he asks of us. This is the work of his creative grace. And so our good Jesus, hearing the words, "I cannot do it; get me out of this", listens to the spirit, the heart made in the image of the Father, knowing that it *can* do it. Being good, he responds to this wordless cry and not to the spoken one.

Looking back over our prayer, *Anima Christi*, we see that we have made a number of very daring petitions. We have asked the soul of Christ to be the animating principle of our life. This is to take on a large responsibility. Being our own animating principle does not ask very much of us, but when *his* spirit is our animating principle? Yes, that is another story! We have begged to be made humble enough to listen to the cautions of the body: "*Corpus Christi, salva me.*" In praying, "O blood of Christ, inebriate me", we have desired to be lifted out of ourselves, to surpass our own possibilities in this sacred inebriation. In asking the water from the side of Christ to wash us, we have pleaded to be made capable of total giving, so that every drop of us flows out upon others. And we have asked that the Passion of Christ should strengthen us and, therefore, petitioned to take on the responsibility of those who have been made strong.

Now we say, "O good Jesus, hear me", which is to entreat: "Do not stop at hearing my words. You are a good Jesus, so listen to the heart that you have made and understand it, although I often do not understand it myself. Listen to the spirit whose capabilities you know because it is the image of your Father with whom you are one." Indeed, he hears more than we can say, sometimes the very opposite of what we say, often enough what we would fear to hear ourselves. He listens to the voice of our own possibilities. He hears and sounds the deeps of our God-given potential. And he answers appropriately.

VII

INTRA TUA VULNERA ABSCONDE ME

Within your wounds, hide me

WE COME NOW in reflecting on the demanding prayer *Anima Christi* to another mystical supplication. "*Intra tua vulnera absconde me*", "Within your wounds, hide me." Religious poets through the centuries have become ecstatic in their expression of this idea. Anyone who has the least semblance of a poet's heart will respond to the sheer beauty of this mystical thought. The fact is, though, that expressions of true mysticism are very real, very practical. The authentic mystics were the most realistic of persons; that is why they were mystics. They were not put off their path, so to speak, by what is passing and ephemeral, by what is superficial, by what is merely apparent. They saw through to the reality of things. If you would ask me for a definition of a mystic, I might say first of all: a realist. And if you would question me as to who are the greatest realists, I would probably want to reply: the greatest mystics.

This is certainly manifest in Saint Francis, to whom holy Church gives a more than arresting adjectival denomination, "seraphic". How can a human being be seraphic? Yet, it is a very appropriate appellation the Church has designated for him. For Francis is on fire as the seraphs are on fire, with love. Again, when the Fathers of the Church loved to tell us of the Church issuing from the side of Christ, they were certainly presenting us with a very mystical expression and, therefore, a very true expression. For when we are told that the Church comes forth from the side of Christ, we are being taught that the Church is born of his love, which from the beginning of mankind has been associated with the heart, the pulsing mid-organ of the body.

Lovers from time immemorial have poetized, dreamed, mused on the heart. "I give you my heart." "You are in my heart." "With all the love of my heart." And, in more modern times, Jesus himself has given us the devotion to his Sacred Heart as the seat of his love. Thus, when we say that the Church issues forth from the side of Christ, we declare that she is born of his love. "Know that I am with you always, yes, to the end of time" (Mt 28:20). He said this, but then he ascended to his Father. He did not remain as the humanly visible incarnate Word of God, but he abides in the Holy Eucharist and is present in the Church, which had first come forth from his love.

Again, when we reflect on the Church coming forth from the side of Christ, we think, of course, of the blood of his heart. We speak of "my heart's blood" when we have given our all, our very last ounce of energy or attention, to a laborious and arduous work. We say, "My heart's blood is in it!" Very truly we can say of holy Church, "His heart's blood is in her." So, in this poetic flight in the midst of the *Anima Christi* prayer, "Within your wounds, hide me", we have indeed an expression of high mysticism that is also of its nature a burningly practical prayer.

What is it that we would hide in a wound? If we ourselves have an open wound, what we want to fold into it is something to heal it, something to soothe its rawness. True enough, part of healing is astringency; but this does not pertain to what is hidden in the wound. By the astringent agent the wound is cleansed. What is hidden in the wound for its healing is something soothing. When we say, "In your wounds, hide me", we present ourselves to Christ as a healing factor in the sufferings of his mystical body.

Looking on the great crucifix in the choir or then at the small one in our cell, we ponder what it means to be hidden in his wounds. And there comes this thought of the healing agent to be hidden in a wound. Is it presumptuous to say, "The Lord revealed it to me"? Rather, we can say humbly that, as a matter of fact, he did, as he always reveals every true understanding we

73

are ever given. Who else would reveal it? So, yes, God gives us to understand that this petition is a love song.

It is not a question in this invocation, "Hide me within your wounds", of my safety in a superficial sense. It is by no means to say, "Fold me into this wound so that I do not need or want to be concerned about anything. I am safe! There is nothing that can trouble me now. I do not have to be involved; I am all enfolded in this wound." No, this is not my wound; it is clear that this is a wound of the crucified Christ. We look at the crucifix and see him there with the open wounds in his nailed hands, in his bleeding feet, with his open side. And do we not feel: I have to do something. Hide me in those wounds. Bring me into them to soothe the wounds of your mystical body which is the Church. Let me be a healing, soothing agent. Make me small enough, a little poor one like Saint Francis, who can be fitted into the wounds of Jesus. Let me not be angular with pride, arrogance, selfishness, but let me be humbly round enough for insertion into the wounds of Christ. Let me not be astringent. Let me not have a caustic tongue, a sharp eye, a harsh word. But let me be the gentle, healing one who brings soothing to the wounds of Christ in his Church. Yes, this prayer is a love song. It is a desire to comfort the Lord.

We can see this quite prominently in the lives of some of the saints, particularly the virgin saints. Remember, for instance, the example of Saint Gertrude, who was unable to look at those nails, those wounds, without taking action. During one Holy Week she took the nails out of her crucifix and put in sweet spices, cloves, instead. Now, there are undoubtedly those, and particularly in our present day, who would throw up their hands and say, "That is just what one would expect of people who talk about brides and bridal love. No reality! Just playing house in the world, living in a dolls' world of fantasy."

Only the truth is: Saint Gertrude was in love. And love always has to do something; love never just sits by. So she did what the worldly minded of a superficially practical world would call nonsense, child's play, silliness. But our Lord revealed to Saint Gertrude that he was consoled by her love. Gertrude had inquired of him, you recall. She wanted to know whether he had noticed what she had done and if he was pleased. He was.

We are taken back in history to the holy women who were, again by earthly standards, doing perfectly useless things. Christ was dead now; what use to bring spices and waste them? He was the outcast of men, and men had done away with him. But the women had to do something. And that something was certainly beyond the ordinary Jewish burial rites. It was something driven by love. They wanted to sing him their love song. Only our Lady really understood, really believed, really knew that he would rise again. These women, although they believed that his death was final and that he would be a living being no more, still had to do something. Love extended beyond death, desiring to give human consolation. We know that they had a great reward: Jesus appeared to them. They had looked after his needs in life, these holy women; they were not about to stop looking after them in death. And because they had set out to do this, they were prepared for an even greater impossibility. They were going to roll away the stone. The fact that it was clearly impossible for women to do this just did not trouble them at all. Somebody they loved was behind that stone, and they were going to roll it away.

In the same way, Saint Mary Magdalen, a frail and battered woman, was to say: "Tell me where you have laid him, and I will take him away (Jn 20:15). She did not even stop at: "I'll get help to take him away." Just, "I will take him away." This is the language of love that worldlings and those who know not of love but only of self-satisfaction will never understand, though every true lover understands it readily enough. Love is always seeking to do the impossible. And one may truly say that love is always in some sense capable of the impossible.

Thus we make, in the midst of the *Anima Christi*, this quite impossible prayer that only a lover will understand. "I must soothe you, I must heal you, I must help you. Hide me in your wounds." We would not want to stop at the invocation: "Hide me!" at a merely superficial consideration of our own safety, our supposed well-being. Indeed, all that will be so when we abide in the wounds of Christ. Truly, we *are* safe, but not in the sense that we are preserved from suffering; rather, we sink down into the midst of suffering. We are hidden in Christ's raw wounds. There is a specific call to each of us to be in all the raw wounds of the Church, in all the agonizing wounds of Christ's mystical body. We must be a healing agent in the raw wounds of Christ's vicar on earth, in the raw wounds of theological pride, of exegetical arrogance, in all the raw wounds on the Church's beautiful face, on the Church's stricken body, on the agonies of the whole world.

When we sincerely sing this love song to Christ, "O hide me in your wounds", we shall achieve a deeper safety than we could have dreamed. It is, in a lover's sense, a very perilous safety. We are safe from delusions, while always in peril of suffering. And what a felicitous peril this is: to be in the peril in which the Son of God always placed himself, in peril of misunderstanding, in peril of betrayal, in peril of denial, in peril of ingratitude, in peril of cavil and plotting, in peril of every human assault. When we are hidden in the wounds of Christ we are safe from danger, but not from the peril in which he chose to situate himself. We cannot ask to be hidden in the wounds of Christ as though sealed off from being wounded ourselves. Rather, hidden in those wounds of Christ, we are safe on a far deeper level—safe from self. Saved unto him, healing him, soothing him, loving him in his mystical body which is the Church.

In this prayer there is nothing of the desire to be aloof, nothing of the spineless wish to be released from pain and suffering and earthly reality, but rather agreement to a very suffering safety. Our blessed Savior was always safe in the love of the Father, always secure in the will of the Father. At the same time, in obeying the Father, Jesus was always in peril of his very life. He was in "danger" of all those things we have just reviewed and many more besides. If we do not want to be in peril of misunderstanding, ingratitude, discouragement, perhaps even of denial and betrayal, of acute disappointment, sometimes precisely from those of whom we had expected much, then we had better not make this prayer. This central phrase of the *Anima Christi* is going to lead us directly into the eternal finale of the prayer. Like all mystical flights, this petition is an arrow of truth. We achieve the safety we seek on a much deeper level than might appear. We are saved from aloofness. We are placed directly at the heart of redemption. "Hide me within your wounds."

With Saint Francis, who likewise bore those wounds upon his precious and frail body, we can have the courage ourselves to make this petition together, to pray that we may be little poor ones who can be hidden in a wound, little kind ones who bring healing to wounds, little gracious-tongued and sweet-visaged persons who bring soothing to the wounds of Christ's mystical body. And if you ask, "But what shall we do when we see ourselves so angular, so astringent, so susceptible to selfish harshness?" the simple answer is: Surrender all these unbeautiful facts about ourselves before the crucifix. What we cannot rid ourselves of by our own puny efforts, we can deliver over to Christ: "Take it!" For this is our good Jesus. He is not there on that Cross saying, "Bring me flowers, I will take them. Bring me fruit, I welcome that. Sing me a lovely song, I enjoy that." This is the good wounded Jesus, who says, "Bring me that pride that you cannot grapple with. Give it up—to me. I shall take care of it." We must pay a price, however, in giving over our pride; we shall be left with the responsibility to be humble. And if we say, "Take away this sharpness and astringency and ungraciousness in me because I am not able to cope with it myself", he will take it. But again we shall be left with the responsibility to be gracious, to be kind, to be amiable, to be sweetly compassionate.

This invocation of the *Anima Christi* invites us to

offer Jesus all that cannot be a healing agent in the wounds of Christ's mystical body—and afterward to bring him what we are left with when he takes all of that away. We need to learn "by heart" the cadence of this love song, "Within your wounds, hide me, Lord." Living in his wounded heart, we attain infinite power to be healing agents of his mystical body, for his own heart is omnipotent to heal the wounds of the world, and his love is infinite.

VIII

NE PERMITTAS ME SEPARARI A TE

Do not allow me to be separated from you

Now in our *Anima Christi* prayer we halt at the petition, "Do not allow me to be separated from you", "*Ne permittas me separari a te.*" The passive form of the verb is very significant. We are not saying to God: "Do not separate me from you", but, "Do not permit me to be separated from you." We are the ones who do the separating. We have in this petition a return to that awesome basic of theology: that we are sovereignly free. An omnipotent God has thought it good to circumscribe his omnipotence with our free will. We can say to this all-powerful God, Yes or No. We can respond to his call, or we can choose not to do so. He has gifted us with an awesome, even terrifying liberty. We can choose to waste our lives, to be mediocre, to go to hell. We can also elect to persevere, to be holy, to live with him forever in eternal bliss. Understanding something of the fearsome dimensions of this freedom, the author of the *Anima Christi* implores, "Do not allow me to do what, left to myself, I will surely do, for then I shall be separated from you."

What we ask for in this prayer is support. We ask God to set up danger signs on his gift of freedom because we fear to misuse it. We plead for structure and discipline. It seems clear that this is a prayer for the sacraments and the power that they bring so that we do not misuse the gift of free will. It is a prayer for structure, in which we ask God to give us laws to stop us from doing what we of ourselves would do. Is not this petition of the *Anima Christi* at the heart of the Israelite's repeated cry given us by the psalmist, "Oh! how I love your law, O Lord!"

We ask for law to help us use our great gift rightly. We ask for support. We petition in one way or another for the support of community, which helps us, invites us, enables us to do what we know, of ourselves, we would not often do. Religious are asking here for the support of their vows in a true giving of themselves totally to God, just as married persons ask divine help to stand firm on the support of their marriage vows. Vows are a receiving of the power to do what God asks us to do. Making a vow of obedience, we receive in the vow the power to obey in a way that we otherwise could not. We made a total surrender of ourselves in the vow of chastity and receive the power of the vow to live in a chastity more perfect than we could attain without the power of the vow. And so with other vows.

When we are asking not to be separated from God, we are begging that he not allow it. "*Ne permittas!*" Do not let me waste and ruin the gift that you have given to me in my free will. Do not let me use it in the wrong way. Do not permit me to be separated from you, for I know that I have the terrible power to be so. I have my freedom. I have the means. But I cry out, "Do not allow this."

What is it that would separate us from Christ? Jesus has told us what he is like. He has said, "I am meek; I am humble of heart" (see Mt 11:29). Therefore, we know that our pride would separate us from him because it is what he is not. We know that our arrogance, our aggressiveness would separate us from him because he has said, "I am gentle and lowly."

Then he has told us that he is the truth. Thus we know that any dishonesty with ourselves before God or others separates us from Jesus, who is the truth. Saint John has revealed to us: "God is love" (1 Jn 4:8). It follows that whatever is unloving in us separates us from Christ. These are the things that he has very specifically told us that he is: meek, humble, all love, truth. And what of the way he functions? How does he act? How does he live?

The first consideration might be his mobility. And

in that, of course, comes flexibility. Jesus is always on the move. We see this as he goes forward in the will of the Father. Often enough we of ourselves are not on the move, except possibly in the wrong direction. We tend to be static. And all sin is static. There is nothing mobile or flexible about sin. It is like the mule that digs its heels in the road and will not move. But Jesus is ever *in via ad Patrem*. One could linger on so many incidents in his life that demonstrate this. Let us look at just a few.

We see him moving on toward Bethlehem in the womb of his mother, from something comfortable and "right" to something more—always something more. And even before that, he had moved forward in the womb of his mother in his first evangelizing, that of John in the womb of his mother, Elizabeth. Jesus moved forward in the service of his mother to what he himself had inspired her to do. We see him notably on the move at twelve, going to the temple and allowing a new phase of his life to unfold there. And when his parents find him and express their sadness that he has caused them such anxiety, he agrees to go back to Nazareth and remain subject to them. We discover him at Cana in the permanence of the divine will declaring that "my hour has not yet come" (Jn 2:4), and yet moving forward in the human decision to advance the hour. A human decision to fulfill a very simple human need. We might have considered multiplying wine depleted by merry-making guests to be a quite unsuitable miracle for Christ to perform, especially as his debut. Jesus moved quickly forward to serve human needs. We tend to sit immobile in the false security of non-action.

We see Christ, above all, in the Garden of Gethsemane, going on when it was agonizing to go on, always on the move into the will of his Father. This is too much; how can I drink this cup? But on he goes. Even before the Garden of Olives, we see him moving forward in the Palm Sunday procession. He beholds that vista of Jerusalem before him from the hill. He sees the golden dome of the temple. And he stops and sobs out loud. That cry is wrenched from his human heart: "Jerusalem, Jerusalem, you that kill the prophets" (Lk 13:34). And the rest of that outcry of anguish: "How often would I have gathered your children together as a hen gathers her brood under her wings, and you would not!" (ibid.). Then, what does he do? Rest in his grief? No. The procession goes on. We need to remember that. Even as our prayer lingers in amazement, love, and compassion with him as he sobs aloud over Jerusalem, we need to remember that he goes on. This is a tremendous truth to reflect upon: forward yet again, whereas we would likely enough have been completely static. The procession went on. And true Christian grief always moves on.

There were many incidents in Jesus' life before that in which he acted when there was, humanly speaking, everything to stop him. There is a colloquial expression that says, "It stopped him cold." That is what often happens to us; we get stopped cold. Jesus did not. He was so warmly mobile in the will of his Father and his love of men that when, for instance, the nine lepers did not even bother to thank him for their cure, he did not stop working miracles for lepers. He went on, even after he revealed to us his profound human hurt. And when his disciples and his apostles disappointed him again and again, he went on. There is Philip asking him strange questions for one who has lived so intimately with the Lord. But while we hear the tiredness in Jesus' voice as he replies, "Have I been with you so long, and yet you do not know me, Philip" (Jn 14:9), we do not find him dissolving the apostolic college. He went on.

We tend to be static, obstinate, obdurate—all the things that separate us from Jesus, who is always on the move. Whereas he was always fixed on the will of his Father, our tendency is to be fixed upon ourselves. But if our eyes are fixed on the Father, we, too, will always be moving *ad Patrem*. We shall be always *in via*, always on the way. Vistas will open out before us. Every sacrifice made will enlarge our view of other sacrifices to be made. Each suffering borne for God will reveal to us more to be suffered and give us strength to suffer more. When there is self-fixation, we become static. When our eyes are fixed on ourselves, we cease to move. We are thus separated from Christ and need to pray for mobility.

This petition immediately evolves into a prayer for faith. We ought never to allow ourselves to forget that Jesus acted and made his painful human decisions as a man and that he did the will of his Father in faith. It is a great mystery, and we cannot fathom it: that this divine will, this divine intellect, was always that of God, and yet Jesus functioned as a man. When, for instance, he made that agonizing decision in the Garden of Olives, he made it as a man to whom the situation appeared unbearable. He foresaw that many would not respond to the love he was pouring out, to the Passion he would undergo. He took, humanly speaking, a great risk. He took a risk on the will of the Father, in faith. I will do your will although it does not seem that this will turn out well, that it is worthwhile. He acted in faith. We are separated from him in the measure that we live on a merely natural plane.

A defective compass needle can point us in the wrong direction. In the spiritual life this happens, too; and it comes of not resisting the impulse to make the merely natural response. Not doing wrong, but simply living on the natural plane so that the needle of our spiritual compass gets off-truth. It points and says,

"This is north." And it is not north. The needle says, "This is the way to happiness." And it is not. The needle says, "This is the way to the fulfillment of your personhood." And it is not. When we live solely on the natural plane, we are separated from Jesus, who was the most perfectly human of all men because he was the most perfect man. But he never lived on the natural plane alone.

All the foregoing small sweep of examples would have elicited a very different response from one living on the merely natural plane, as we can so easily do. He could have said to the doctors of the law in the temple, "I am going to stay here now. I have a lot more to tell you. I have been asking questions; now I shall answer them myself." At Cana, he could have said, "They have had enough." Why should he have to call on his divine power to give them more wine? And why had it run out so fast? They had probably drunk too much too quickly. He would never have gone on to cure more lepers if he had remained on the natural plane of thinking: "That is the thanks I get!" when only one out of ten thought to thank him. And certainly in the Garden of Gethsemane on the natural plane alone he would never have gone on. None of the Gospel paradoxes, either, makes any sense on the natural plane.

So, we are making our prayer for mobility in praying, "*Ne permittas me separari a te.*" We do not want to be separated from Christ on the move. And we pray for faith because we do not want to be separated from Jesus by living just on the natural plane. Out of this, again, comes a prayer for constancy. For it was not that Jesus was on the move sometimes, that he responded in faith occasionally or even frequently. It was always. We pray to be delivered from fickleness, from the languid attitude that "I will do what at this moment seems comfortable to do", even though we have discovered often enough to our suffering, shame, and penance afterward that what we were convinced was so good for us was really for our destruction. When we live by our fickleness instead of by constancy, we are separated from Jesus, the "always" Person, the constant One.

Francis Thompson has a poignant and astute poem about a child who was petulant and fickle. "Why do you so clasp me and draw me to your knee? I will be loved but now and then and when it pleases me." The poet comes to his climax: "So I heard a young child, a thwart child, a young child, rebellious against love's arms, make its foolish cry." And he ends with a plea for forgiveness: "Pardon, Love most high,/ for I think those arms were even Thine, and that child was even I."[1] Is this not often enough true of us who have attained a taller physical stature? We prefer to be given grace to see and grace to amend "now and

[1] *Poems of Francis Thompson*, ed. Rev. Terence L. Connolly (New York, London: D. Appleton-Century Co., 1941), pp. 114-15.

then, and when it pleases me". I will respond to the call to sacrifice when it suits me. I will love when I am in the mood to love. I will let you love me, God, in all these calls to be on the move, to live in faith, to be sacrificial, but only now and then and when it pleases me.

Jesus did the will of the Father when it was not at all pleasing to his human nature. It was not pleasing, even long before the Passion, to be treated with ingratitude, to be disappointed again and again, to receive such small returns for his love. But he did the will of the Father always and not just when it was agreeable to his humanity.

Out of that constancy comes directly that persevering love absolutely characteristic of Jesus. Saint John says of him that, "having loved his own who were in the world, he loved them to the end" (Jn 13:1). Again, we see in ourselves, flowing right out of the previous consideration, a sometimes-love, a self-centeredness. Christ was always Father-centered and other-centered. It is when we are focused on ourselves that we have sometimes-love. When we look back on our own lives, we realize that we have sometimes experienced that feeling of, "What's the use?" in situations, particularly at times with persons. And yet there is that unquenchable love that God has put in our hearts, which comes up like a tide and against all evidence to the contrary. It urges us to say, "No, I will try again."

This is what we want to nurture in ourselves. This is of Christ. It is the always-love.

This persevering, constant love, like mobility and the faith response, comes out of suffering and pain. The love that is not persevering, the sometimes-love that separates us from Christ, is a matter of emotions, situations, persons, circumstances, surprises. But the persevering love of Jesus is the unquenchable love. And this is what we are praying for in the *Anima Christi* when we beg, "Do not allow me to be separated from you." Jesus, you are always on the move toward your Father; deliver me from the bad choice of free will to sit down and be obstinate, obdurate, static. It is a prayer for faith: "Do not permit me to live on a merely natural plane." It is a plea for constancy: "Do not permit me to be separated from you by my own fickleness; do not allow me to say to you, 'I will be loved, but now and then and when it pleases me.'" It is a prayer for persevering love against sometimes-love. And encompassing all of these, returning to our prefatory remarks, this petition is a great cry for support. It is a plea for what many do not like, but for what God likes: structure. There is structure in all that he has made, including ourselves.

On the very obvious level of physical life, we need support so that we are not separated from Christ. It is a beautiful thing to rise in the middle of the night to pray; but I wonder how long any of us would do that without the support of the bell, without the support of all the other sisters rising with us? I am not sure. It is a good thing to be austere in our diet, to take whatever is offered. Yet I wonder how many of us would faithfully be there at the same time, whether we felt like it or not, to take always whatever is set before us whether we liked it or not, unless we had the support of the community doing this with us? I wonder who among us would go to prayer again and again and again at those specified times during the day without the support of community? And so it is in family life, indeed, in any Christian vocation.

Then, on the very profound spiritual level, who will dare to say that she can be perfectly obedient without the supporting power of vows? Who can aspire to be completely chaste, completely loving, without the strengthening support of a vow of chastity? Who will say that she will be poor, a little one of God, without the power of a vow of poverty? Our weakness always invites us to wander off; and who will say that she will always be content in a little space with God, unless she has the power of her vow of enclosure? Or who, in conjugal love, can be assured of chaste fidelity without the stout anchoring of marriage vows?

This daring prayer says: You have given me this tremendous, almost incomprehensible gift, almighty God, enabling me with my free will to be so powerful that I can say Yes or No to you. I will respond to you, or I will not. I will be on the move all the time, or I will sit down. I will live in faith, or I will live on the natural plane. I will be constant, or I will be fickle. I will persevere in unquenchable love, or I will settle for a sometimes-love. God offers us the power, the support needed to make right choices. This is what we beg when we pray: "Do not permit me to be separated from you." Give me to live as one empowered to live fully, which is to say, united to you in all things at all times.

IX

AB HOSTE MALIGNO DEFENDE ME

From the evil enemy, defend me

THERE ARE SOME DEFENSES that must be thrown up if we are not to be separated from Christ, if we are to be on the move with Jesus and totally given to him. And so we ask him now, in this petition of the prayer, to defend us from the evil enemy. *"Ab hoste maligno defende me."*

"Maligno" is truly a terrible word. It is not just any enemy from whom we ask to be shielded. Enemies roam a wide expanse and are of varying intensities. There are little enemies that attack us rather like swarms of gnats. There are larger enemies, mostly of our own construction. But then there is the really evil enemy, *"hostis malignus"*. We know how we use that word: malignant, evil, something destructive. On the physical plane we are all too familiar in our times with malignancy. A person has a malignant growth, a cancerous tumor. What is a malignant growth? It is a

wild, undisciplined growth of cells always bearing destruction as its message, its business, its goal. A wild growth of malignant cells in the body, the blood, the brain, is out for destruction. And so is evil in all its forms.

Christian philosophers are fond of telling us that evil does not exist. They rightly remind us that, philosophically, evil is the absence of a due good. But there is a pseudo-philosophy in our times that would have us believe that evil does not exist in the sense that everything is good, that man is incapable of wrong, that he just wanders about from good to good, getting better all the time. This is rather obviously without a substantial file of examples. But we consider here the true philosophy with its precise definition of evil as the non-presence of good. Evil is of its nature that which is not, exactly because it is the absence of a due good. Evil is that which is not, the uncreated, because God is Creator, and God creates only what is good. "And God saw everything that he had made, and behold, it was very good" (Gen 1:31). It is the distortion of his good that is supremely wrong and completely evil, wholly distorted when there is a total absence of good.

Evil has not an existence of itself. Its business is destruction. And, like physical malignancy, destroying good is its work and scope. Evil is everything that God is not. It is everything that God has not created;

evil is distortion to the point of deception. It is the lie. Our blessed Savior said, "I am . . . the truth" (Jn 14:6). Evil is the negation of truth, without reality in itself, but rather the absence of that reality which is the good. Therefore, malignancy of the soul would of necessity have pretenses as its expressions, since evil is the lie. It can never have any expression of itself except some form of untruthfulness. From that base, we can look into the nature of this evil enemy under the three headings that all classic spiritual writers, the Fathers of the Church, and before them the very Scriptures have presented to us. We know what they are: the world, the flesh, and the devil.

First, then, the world. In what way does the world present itself to us as the *"hostis malignus"* from which we beg Jesus to defend us? In what way is it the lie? We know the scriptural distinction in the two ways we speak of the world. There is the sense in which our Lord said that he was not of this world and that his kingdom was not of this world. That is the world of which we now speak, not adverting here to the other sense of the world—that good world of God's creation which is our place of exile but in so many ways an extraordinarily beautiful place in which to be exiled. We are considering here "the world" that is anti-God and in which his kingdom has no place, that world of which Christ spoke when he said to his apostles, "If you were of the world, the world would love its own; but because you are not of the world, but I chose you out of the world, therefore the world hates you" (Jn 15:19). When we speak of the evil enemy of the world in this scriptural sense, there are at least three captions under which we can consider this evil and how it presents itself to us.

The first lie that the world tells us is that it is a lasting city. We know from Holy Scripture that "here we have no lasting city" (Heb 13:14). And the malignant evil of the world in this first pretension is to say that the world does and will endure. Once we subscribe, even in small measure, to this deception, all things assume a disproportion. If the world is our lasting city, ipso facto and *instanter*, our values are changed. The world keeps insisting, "I am what endures. Pitch your tent here. Put your roots down in me." Once we lose our healthy sense of the world as a lovely stopping-off place, but passing, fading and ephemeral, once we lose the sense that we are pilgrims *in via ad Patrem*, as Saint Francis and Saint Clare and all the saints understood so well, and clasp it to ourselves as a lasting city, all things are distorted. From this first lie of the world, that we have here a lasting city, we ask Jesus to defend us in this petition of the *Anima Christi* prayer.

The second lie of the malignant evil of the world is the assurance that the world is what matters. It is to be grasped, to be held on to. If it tells us first that it is a

97

lasting city, it maintains as its second great deception that it is all there is. It is not only that the world insists, "I last", but that it also declares, "I am all that is important. Get as much of me as you can and hold me tightly in your grasp." This is to miss the whole point of Christ's message, which was so clear in the hearts of Francis and Clare. They enjoyed the good world as the setting of their lives precisely because they never sought to own it.

We combat this malignant lie of the world's supreme importance by letting the rose die. Saint Francis loved the fragrance of the rose, but he would never have wanted it not to lose its petals. For it is the destiny of the rose to bloom, to give joy, to give fragrance, and to die. This is the point to remember: let the rose die. If we do not grasp at things that are by their very nature ephemeral, then we will not grasp at ourselves, at what we think to be our own rights, our own designs, as if we were not destined to die. Rather, every day should be death. We are moving steadily toward the death that ushers us into eternity. But there should also be a daily dying to all that is not good in us, all that is not Jesus in us. Let it be! Let the rose die. In the little situations of every day, let our petals fall. Let us allow ourselves to go to the Lord.

The third lie of the world is that it is the appearance of things that is important, the surface that matters. Thus the world can tempt us to exchange reality for appearance to the extent that we find ourselves (or, worse, perhaps do not find ourselves) living on the periphery of our own life. We can spin flightily along through our whole lives without ever really situating ourselves at the center that is Christ. We can stand on the shore of our own life instead of plunging into its waters. The more we live by the worldly dictum of superficiality, by what appears rather than by what is, the more we are in the clutches of this *hostis malignus*. That is why we pray that Jesus will defend us from the great lies of the world: that it is a lasting city, that it is all there is, and that what appears on the surface is reality.

Then to look at the second enemy: the flesh. What we may tend to think of first and perhaps exclusively is the lust of the flesh, the carnal passions that can be so insistent in their efforts to dominate us. These truly become great evils if we do not combat them, but there are more subtle evils of the flesh than these. Perhaps the initial one is acedia, as the classical writers have called it. Acedia, the sloth of the spirit, the lassitude of the *anima*. Lassitude takes two forms. For the evil of acedia, its lie, is two-headed. A two-horned demon, if you prefer. There is, first, lassitude per se, that wish not to rouse ourselves to make spiritual effort. Once we yield to that, we certainly will not bestir ourselves to much physical effort, either. This lassitude, which enervates us if we allow ourselves to succumb to it, is the lie of the flesh that says, "Take it easy. Give as little as you can. Just make it. Why put yourself out?" Acedia, sloth of the spirit. It is a vicious and malignant temptation. But the other horn of this evil enemy is a bustle of activity, also a form of acedia. That is, we charge about and race around in order to avoid the real work of the spirit. We try to justify in activity our lack of spiritual effort. Or we simply indulge our self-will by doing, with a great outpouring of energy, just what we wish to do, and this as a camouflage for a lack of genuine effort on the part of the spirit. So, the first malignant lie of the flesh is acedia. Take it easy. Do as little as possible. Or, raise a lot of dust and accomplish so much outwardly that there is no need to work spiritually. You are justified by output.

The second lie of the flesh is in its pretense that it is the center and that everything must serve its needs. This, of course, begets that overindulgence of the appetites which is ruinous in any form of life. It is this of which Saint Teresa of Avila spoke in her usual forthright way when she said, "What have you come here for?—to have the longest life possible?" We must face this humbly. It is entirely possible, after having set out precisely to cast our life away into the arms of God, as Saint Francis and Saint Clare and all the saints so well knew how to do, that we can become extremely concerned about ourselves and to make our poor flesh the center of our lives. We become dominated by the flesh, urgently concerned about its least demand or its smallest debility. And so our whole life gets off-center. The flesh can be such a good servant and one to be reverenced. But it is not the center of our lives, not the dominant note in our song. Against the lie that it is the center and dominant, we ask our Lord to defend us.

Out of this flows the third lie of the flesh, which seems to be the opposite of the second but is actually very closely related to it. According to this deception, the flesh should not be reverenced. It is simply a miserable vehicle of which the soul must take some notice but which can be treated contemptuously. It should not be reverenced, this lie argues, for it is not of any particular importance, just a vehicle of mobility and a necessary cabinet for the soul. Far from making us "spiritual", however, this attitude leads to many dissipations and an all-encompassing coarseness of soul. The more irreverent we are to physical things, particularly our own bodies, the cruder of soul we become. Nor shall we find exceptions to this. We do not respect the spirit if we do not reverence the flesh. So, there are the three lies of the flesh: acedia, lassitude, ease; off-centeredness, "I am all that matters" (and this so akin to the second lie of the world); or "I am nothing. Treat me crudely. I am not to be reverenced, but despised. I am, per se, the enemy." No, the flesh is not per se the enemy. The lies of the flesh are the evil enemy from which we beg to be delivered in this prayer.

The devil, too, has three malignant lies to tell us and to which he untiringly solicits our subscription. The first, of course, has to do with ambition. The fall of the archangels of God: "*Non serviam!*" I will not serve. Ambition and disobedience. I will not bow my head. This lie leads us to neglect all the Gospel paradoxes, which tell us, If you want to keep your life, throw it away (see Mt 10:39). If you want to be exalted (and everyone made in the image of God should healthily want to be exalted), humble yourself (see Lk 14:11). If you want to make yourself the highest, then become the least (see Lk 9:48). And so on. We know that the Gospels abound in paradoxes. Ambition gives the lie to all this. It says, No, this is not true. *Non serviam!* I must dominate. I must have my way. I must save my own life. I must lord it over others. *Non serviam* is the first lie the devil himself spoke, and in speaking those words he became, no longer Lucifer, the light-bearer, but the devil, Satan, the liar.

The second of the devil's malignant lies has to do with rationalization. This is the lie he proposed to our first parents: But why not this tree? Does that make sense? Why does God say that you may eat of all the other trees, but not this one? (see Gen 3:1). Anyone can see that this tree is just as beautiful and good as the others, just as healthy. Why is God so eccentric? Why not this tree? Is God afraid of something? You will be like God! The devil gave the lie to the word of God in the Scriptures telling us, "My thoughts are not your thoughts, neither are your ways my ways" (Is 55:8). It does not matter if this tree looks like all the others or if it seems even to excel all the others in life-giving qualities, in beauty, in nutrition. I am God, and I say, You shall not eat of this tree. You shall not rationalize. My word suffices. Thou shalt not.

We know how easily the lie of rationalization can intrude itself into our daily lives. We cannot rationalize obedience. We cannot rationalize God. Out of that second malignant deception of the devil flows immediately his third lie: pretense. "You will be like God" (Gen 3:5). You shall be perfect; you shall be blameless. The devil is all pretense, and everything in our lives that is in any way pretentious is a subscribing to the third malignant lie of the devil. Any pretension we let assume dominance in our life delivers us up to that "*hoste maligno.*"

And so we pray together to Jesus, our Lord and Love, that he defend us from the evil enemy of the world, the flesh, and the devil, all of them liars from the beginning, but not proof against a humble heart humming with the name of Jesus and determined to do always the things that please him.

X

IN HORA MORTIS MEAE VOCA ME, ET JUBE ME VENIRE AD TE

In the hour of my death, call me and bid me come to you

And so we come to the final phrases of the prayer *Anima Christi*. It seems clear that the petition "*In hora mortis meae, voca me*", "In the hour of my death, call me", cannot be separated from what follows: "*et jube me venire ad te*", "and bid me come to you." While the prayer is immediately concerned with that final call which is death, the same thing is true of every one of God's calls in our lives. There is never a call for no particular reason; every call is in fact for the very same reason.

God calls us at our birth; God calls us at our death. God calls us every day of our lives. And for one reason only: that we should come to him. So, instead of beginning with a consideration of that final call of death, perhaps we would do better first to reflect on God's calling us into life. Not "*hora mortis meae*", but "*hora nativitatis meae*", the hour of my birth when he called me from my mother's womb into the outer expression of an individual life of my own upon this earth. That first call into life was for one reason: that I should come to him. And whenever a life is wasted or distorted, it is invariably because that call to come to God was not understood or was left unanswered.

Often enough God's calls impose on us human suffering, human pain. We see this already and quite dramatically in our first call "*in hora nativitatis meae*", the call of our birth. What does the child do when called from the repose of the womb? Well, it cries its little heart out. This, of course, is a healthy sign of life; but it is also a sign that the baby objects to having its repose disturbed for the harder life of light and noise and many strange, new elements. Francis Thompson, in one of his most exquisite poems for the children of Wilfrid and Alice Meynell, "The Making of Viola", muses on this. We wait with great joy for this lovely child to appear. Then the child comes forth. And cries. The poet mourns, "Our first gift to you is a gift of tears, poor Viola!"[1]

Something of this is in every call we hear, because every one of God's calls asks us to go forward to something in one sense less restful than what we had before, simply by reason of being a forward movement,

[1] *Poems of Francis Thompson*, ed. Rev. Terence L. Connolly (New York, London: D. Appleton-Century Co., 1941), p. 14.

a growth. Something, too, of the distress of the new-born infant called from the comfortable and unde-manding shade of the womb into a more personal and quite demanding way of living persists throughout life in our answering God's calls. We never go forward without effort. We can coast only downward, never upward and clearly not forward. We never move ahead without suffering in some degree.

As the infant grows, it receives repeated calls to maturity, to reason. It learns to form words, and that is a call to learn the language of God. It learns with help to walk, to take steps forward; and already there is the call of God to walk that straight road to him, really the basic reason for learning how to walk. We know how a parent encourages the little one in its toddling walk by standing at a distance with outstretched arms, and how the tiny child intuits that the summons to walk— a very difficult procedure!—is for the purpose of ar-riving in the arms of the parent. It makes all the difference to the infant. Again, returning to speech, it is the Word of God that is the reason for mastering speech. We want to learn the language of God, and we want to walk a straight road to the Father.

We are most fully alive when we are coming most directly to God. We are least alive when we are least responsive to God's calls, from his first call into life to his multitudinous other invitations through life, when we are rambling off on byways, following little tortuous paths of self. We are not responding when we are wandering off away from grace even though God is calling us to come forward on a direct path to him. The straight path of grace begins with tears, is continued with tears in some measure, and usually ends with the tears of death, however willing and even sweet those final tears may be, tears of the dying one and notably the tears of those loving the dying one. But this, too, God has described in the Scriptures when he explains that heaven is the state where, when we have answered the final call and come to him forever, he wipes all tears from our eyes. What a stark reminder the poet Father Alfred Barrett, S.J., has given us: "If heaven will be the banishing of tears,/ There must be tears for God to wipe away." [2]

After the call of birth, there is that second major call: the call into Christianity and into Catholicism, which some of us received as infants and others heard later in life. Again, it is a call to come to God. The call to Christianity, the call into the Catholic Church, is not a call to membership in a prestigious international establishment. It is not a call to keep specific laws per se. It is not a call to join a society that offers us a certain security. No, it is a call to walk more directly, more securely, more firmly to God. "*Jube me venire ad te.*" Let me come to you! It is this to which God gives

[2] Father Alfred Barrett, S.J., *Mint by Night* (New York: America Press, 1938), p. 46.

assent when he calls us into baptism, to come more directly to him in a life of faith with the strength of the sacraments. We can walk so much better with them. We have strength. So our great call from God into his Church is not to membership in a worldwide society of considerable standing, but a call to come to him with means to do that more directly, a little faster, and much more securely.

For Poor Clares, a call to Franciscan religious life has followed. And this, too, is a call to come to God. Again, it is not a call for any other basic reason. Not a call to enrollment in what even the world rather acknowledges as a generally pleasant company. It is a familiar saying that "the whole world loves Saint Francis", and the magnificent truth of the saying pulls at our hearts. However, what has been received is not just an invitation to be a part of a great, idealistic society that he established and rooted so firmly and so simply in the gospel, but a call to live like the meek and humble Christ, as Francis did. Like him, we are called by Jesus to be lowly. And why? Because the Franciscan Order was described by its founder as the society of the very least ones in the Church of God? No. Rather, his followers are called to be the lowly ones in the Church of Christ because Christ himself was meek and lowly and humble of heart. And the call to his way of life is a call to come very directly to the meek and humble Christ.

Again, there is a call to be obediently poor because Christ was obediently poor. It is a summons to be thought of little worth by worldly standards, just as Christ was. "Can anything good come out of Nazareth?" (Jn 1:46). How could anything good have come out of little Assisi, forever struggling with its petty wars? Yet, Nazareth is remembered only because one Person was a Nazarene, just as Assisi is famous because Francis and Clare lived there, and hardly for any other reason. Nazareth doubtless would have been well forgotten except that Jesus the Nazarene abode and prayed and worked there. And Assisi would assuredly have been highly unremembered save that Francis and Clare were born there and heard there a call to come to God in the hour of their youth. After the *"hora nativitatis meae"* comes the *"hora juventutis meae"*, the hour of my youth when I am called into vitalizing faith, into the fullness of Catholicism.

Then, we have our Christian call to be lighthearted and joyous because Christ has invited us to leave all things for him and promised us a hundredfold reward even in this life. This is definitely something to sing about. It concerns not merely joining a company of good-natured people called Christians but a profound call to an all-pervasive lightheartedness. And by that we mean that God has called us to live each in his own way like Christ: a simple, evangelical life, poor and humble, obedient to God and Church, cheerfully given and giving, joyful because we are coming very directly to him who was all of these things when he walked our earth.

We are asked as Christians to leave behind, in some sense, our parents, our family, our friends in order to come to him solely, not because the others are of no worth, but because they are of such great worth that we would go beyond them only for him. And in that sense we already receive the promised hundredfold in answering our call to come directly to him, for all things are found in him and found more fully than they were ever before possessed. For example, we find in answering this call to come totally to God that we discover love of our earthly family and friends on a deeper level. We find them in him. We love more tenderly than ever before because we find at a deeper level whomever and whatever we have left for his sake: we find them in him, where they have their own truest meaning and their own fullness of being. It follows very logically that the more directly we answer that call to come to Christ, the more fully do we discover all those we love, since their own being and meaning are in him. Outside of him, we can never fully know our own, much less possess them in love.

Again, there is a call to leave our will. Not to drop it as something of little worth or an impediment to spiritual progress, but to surrender this most precious gift of God back to him who gave it, that we may cling to him. Saint Clare describes this response as that of "a poor virgin clinging to the poor Christ". God does not call us to give up our will as a kind of fitness test for holiness. No, the invitation to surrender our will to the Father is the call to follow Christ, who bent his own human will to the will of the Father. It is just that: a call. And one that he himself answered from the hour of his birth: "Then I said, 'Behold, I have come to do your will, O God,' as it is written of me in the roll of the book" (Heb 10:7), until the hour of Gethsemane: "Not my will, but yours, be done" (Lk 22:42), and on to the consummation of the redemption: "Into your hands I commit my spirit" (Lk 23:46).

The common denominator of every call of God to us from birth to death is the call to come to him. "In the hour of my death, call me." For what reason? That I may come to you. Bid me come to you. *"Jube me venire ad te."* That is the whole point. All of these calls through life on to death must be answered on a very deep, personal level. The call of those of us baptized in infancy was answered in our name by others; but it became a real, living, driving force in our lives, a practical vital force, as we grew to maturity and actuated that decision in ourselves. The infant does not decide to be born and, if consulted, might well indicate his preference for remaining in the undemanding dark repose of the womb. But as the child grows, he must answer his own call to life. Some persons do not. We need to look into ourselves and discover how fully we are answering our call into life so that we may come to God. There is no other reason to have been called into life.

It is the failure to understand life as a call from the Creator into life that leads godless philosophers to despair. We can easily see why that should be so. For if we are called into a life that will end, that has an absolute terminal point, how shall we live it? This is the reason for hedonism, debauchery, despair: this explains all of that company because there has been a call into life understood only as something fleeting and often enough painfully inflictive and afflictive even in its brevity rather than as a call to come to God. Thus, the beautiful call itself becomes a dark summons into a welter of meaninglessness. Even the loveliness of life becomes unbearable to the human heart unable fully to enjoy it because that heart is convinced that beauty is doomed to fade and die. And so nothing beautiful can really be savored, since it is felt to have no meaning outside itself. Everything becomes tainted with despair. Why should we be alive? Why were we called into life at all? It is that we may come to him. Why called to faith in baptism? In order to come to him more securely and with sacramental strength. Why called into Christian living? To come immediately to God in a simple gospel life.

And then there is the final call to death. We should never be tempted to think, "Well, how do I respond to that? There is no choice at all." If I had no choice about emerging from the womb of my mother, one would almost say I have still less choice about death. I cannot say to God: "I do not choose to die" or "I prefer not" or "Not today." Where is the choice? Well, it is at the deepest level, for it is truly a terrible thing to die not choosing to die. We can make a decision in our own death: we can freely agree to the moment and the manner. We can agree to respond to the call. It is not that we are just "stopped" from earthly life or that life is turned off, but that we use the great power of our God-given free will to respond to that call and say: "Yes, now bid me come to you." We could, of course, choose to say, as some do, "No! no! no! I will not die. I do not wish to die. I do not want to come to you. I desire to live longer on earth." Or, "I want to live on earth forever."

There is a tremendous and ultimate choice in death. It is the greatest choice of all—to choose God's appointed moment of our death as our own choice, to assent freely to the manner of our death, to choose in his choice all the circumstances of the death, sudden or prepared for by a long illness, indoors or outdoors, by night or by day, alone or with loved ones around us. We do not know, but we can decide to choose all of that. Saint Pius X had a prayer to which he granted an indulgence, a prayer of his own that he prayed every day. "Right now, I choose with all my heart the circumstances of my death and its hour." Death is not at all the moment and the hour of non-choice. It is the hour of deepest choice. And it flows out of all our other responses to all our other calls to come to God.

And there are the continuing daily calls. With each one of them—to be generous, to give, to spend ourselves—there is the invitation to come to God, who "having loved his own who were in the world, . . . loved them to the end" (Jn 13:1) and in fullest measure, even to the last drop of his blood. Every daily call to suffering is a call to come to him who bore all our infirmities and took all our wounds upon himself (Is 53:4–6). Each daily invitation to patience is an invitation to come to him who was led like a lamb to the slaughter (Is 53:7).

If only we could actuate this right thinking in answering our daily calls, we would widen a spiritual horizon, a vista so beautiful. It is not a matter of God's saying, "I want this sacrifice right now. I wish this suffering right now. I demand this act of obedience right now." And that is the peroration. No, rather, he is asking for an act of obedience, that we may come closer to him who did always the will of his Father. He is asking for patience, that we may come to him who bore all our infirmities without complaint. He is suggesting some particular act of charity, that we may

114

come into the arms of him whose name is Love (1 Jn 4:8). He is offering an opportunity for meekness and humility, that we may deepen our communication with Jesus, who is meek and humble of heart. He is asking this act of self-despoliation that we may be stripped of all things like Christ, who hung upon a Cross stripped of all things, without support, without alleviation. This is what we mean by "call". Not a call to do this or to do that, to suffer this or to give up that, but always a call to come to God.

Thus, we come to pray, "In the hour of my death, call me", knowing that he will, and for the same reason that he has called me all during my life: that I may come to him. We shall be able to make that final decision to say, "Yes! yes! I choose this hour for my death, so that I may come to you", if we have prepared for it by a lifetime of understanding what it means to be called. Do we not see this even in our dealings with one another? If I call one of you, it is for a reason, maybe even the dearest of reasons: just that I want to see you! And when God calls us, it is for a reason, particularly in that dearest final call, which will be made because he just wants to see us. We can help one another remember, by our manner of living, that God has always the same elemental reason for each of his calls, whether in life or in death: that we may come to him.

This is what we want to do: understand every call.

It makes all the difference, because we are so frail and so limited. We get tired of obeying all the time. We get weary of making sacrifices. We lose a taste for penance easily enough. Shamefacedly we must admit that we tire spiritually very, very easily. Unless we re-member that the calls to obedience, to sacrifice, to penance are calls to come to him whom we love. Sometimes it seems a rocky road for the coming, and with hurdles to take. Yet, God is not saying, "I have set up this obstacle course; and I want to see how you do on the rocks, how you jump the hurdles." No, he is calling us to come to him—so what if there are rocks of one kind or another that will have to be suffered, hurdles that will have to be cleared if we are going to get to him? If we understand that we are *in via*.

It is such a precious thing to be called by our name. When as children we were called by name to come in, even though we did not want to come in, there was yet something very intriguing about hearing the sound of our own name. And to think of being called by God with the sound of our own name and in order to come to him! We could be called by others for worthy and substantial reasons or for selfish reasons, ulterior motives, worldly considerations; but God's call, whether into life, into faith in baptism, into our vocation in life, or into each daily situation, is never ulterior, never by-the-way, but always and only that we may come to him.

It is in this particular petition within the *Anima Christi* prayer that we find the meaning and purpose of every other call. Knowing that we are called to the God who loves us is what sweetens every sacrifice, gives meaning to all suffering, infuses pain with splendor. It is the being called that gives significance to human love as well and offers impetus to the mortifications life continually puts before us. If we could only remember that God is calling us by name in the unfolding circumstances of each day, we would assuredly reply: "Yes! Bid me come to you." It is not a case of, "Yes, I will make this sacrifice." Or, "Yes, I will be patient; yes, I will suffer this." There can be more than a bit of vainglory in that. There can be any amount of pride in that. But we come to understand that the call does not end any more than it began in the pain, the suffering, the sacrifice, the mortification, the situation, or the hour of death. It is God who is our Alpha and Omega; he is the common denominator of every call. It is God who is the Caller and the Meaning and the End. If we use our God-given energies to remember this as we respond to the daily calls of our life, then "*in hora mortis nostrae*" we shall be able to reply to that call, too, making in that tremendous, dramatic final hour of our life on earth a deeply personal decision.

XI

UT CUM SANCTIS TUIS LAUDEM TE IN SAECULA SAECULORUM

That, with your saints, I may praise you forever and ever

IT IS THE *"Jube me venire ad te"*, "Bid me come to you", which explains the reason for each of God's calls to us. In every call to sacrifice, to generosity, to charity, to humility, to anything at all, our Lord calls only that we may come to him. If we do not understand this in life, we shall not understand it in death; and that final call will not be fulfilled in our own free choice and response.

Out of that consideration flows the final invocation of this great prayer. The foregoing petition itself explains to us what we are supposed to do when we come to Christ. "Call me and bid me come to you." And then what? So "that with all your saints I may praise you forever and ever". *"Ut cum sanctis tuis laudem te in saecula saeculorum."*

Praise is clearly one of the predominant themes of Holy Scripture and is certainly preeminent in the psalms. It would be an engrossing and rewarding work to go through the psalms searching for their invitations to praise. They luxuriantly abound. There is even a special group of psalms called "the praise psalms". And if this theme runs so strongly, vibrantly, vividly through all of psalmody, it reaches its resounding climax in the final psalms. The last one of them all, Psalm 150, goes quite wild with praise. Reaching the end of psalmody, we have lived with the psalmist through some very hard times and some very downcast days. We have searched God's ways with the psalmist, recognized his complaints as frequently our own, brooded with him on injustice and been ashamed with him in our sins and failings. What, then, is the climax, the final word? "Praise! praise! praise!" Psalm 150 calls us to get out our cymbals, take up our timbrels, set out our harps, and praise, praise, praise!

It is this theme of praise to which the Old Testament as well as the New return us again and again. Some very familiar phrases come immediately to mind. "May the living God, my Savior, be praised forever." Right there is the final phrase of the *Anima Christi* prayer—praise, forever and ever. "*Ut cum sanctis tuis laudem te in saecula saeculorum.*" This praise is never to end. Again, the psalmist tells us that "a sacrifice of praise will give me glory." Does praising seem a rather bland occupation to be engaged in for all eternity? *In saecula saeculorum. Amen?* Let us look into the theme of praise on the human level.

When we love someone very, very much, is it not true that one of our greatest joys is to praise him or her? Another outstanding joy we experience when we love deeply is in hearing the loved one praised. We are pleased to hear others say kind and laudatory words about someone whom we ourselves greatly esteem. There is a very particular joy in this; and the more deeply we love, the deeper is the satisfaction. The more profound our love, the more we wish to hear these praises of the loved one sounded by others as well as by ourselves. What delights a young man in love so much as endlessly extolling the beauty of his loved one? He rehearses and reviews her grace, her virtue, her physical beauty. He enjoys thinking about this, he delights to talk about it, and he loves to hear her praised by others. Or, turning the situation about, what do the poetry of the ages and the music of the centuries and the paintings of the millennia testify that the young girl in love wants to do? She wishes to praise her beloved because he is so handsome, so strong, so upright, so kind, so talented, so brave. This is her joy: to praise.

As love grows stronger, so does the desire to praise increase. It is always a sign of the weakening of love when we have less taste for praising a loved one. This is a good point of spiritual examen. If our love for God is growing less fervent and ardent, we have an inbuilt barometer to warn us. It registers less concern for praising him. No, it is definitely not a rather bleak activity for all eternity, simply to praise. For one thing, the more we love a human being, and certainly the more we grow in the love of God, the more do we see to praise.

The person who loves very little does not see much to praise in the other. Again, this is a test of our charity. If we do not observe much to praise in our neighbor, one thing is certain: we do not know him well enough, love him well enough. If we come to love him more, we shall have our own reward of seeing more and more to praise. The heart that loves little always sees little or perhaps even nothing to praise. The heart that loves much will see something to praise where others may not. But there are qualities and characteristics of praise.

Praise is always humble. This is prominently its very first attribute, because in praising another we in some way situate ourselves below that person. Praise of its nature exalts the one praised, sets this respected person or this dear God or this loved friend above the one praising. By the mere act of praising, we assume a position of humility. We take a willing stance beneath another person. We claim the position so favored by Saint Francis and Saint Clare, that of being prostrate at the feet of God and at the feet of others. There is the first property of praise. It is, of its nature, humble.

Turning our consideration around, we can hardly fail to observe that in reality the less humble we are, the less taste we shall have for praising others and the less we shall understand the glory of having an eternal activity, eternal assignment, to praise God. The humbler we are, the more ardent grows our desire to praise. And the more we truly praise, the more do we discover how much there is to praise. This *in saecula saeculorum* praising of God is not static but forever unfolding, the horizons endlessly expanding.

The second characteristic of praise is assuredly that it is joyous. The one who praises is by the very act, not grudging, but spontaneous and eager. We sometimes hear the description that a critic, perhaps a drama critic, maybe a music critic, often enough an everyday-life critic, gave "grudging praise" to someone or to a performance. This is no praise at all. Praise of its nature can never be grudging, but must be joyously, freely given. It flows out of desire. I would venture to say that it flows out of need. Humbly situated beneath it, we see something praiseworthy, and we *must* praise it. There is spontaneity, eagerness. This, of course, was so very characteristic of Saint Francis and Saint Clare. They saw more and more to praise. We have Francis' *Canticle of the Creatures*: "O dear Lord, be praised for the sun! Be praised—you made the moon! Be praised—you created fire so ardent! Be praised—you made the water so lovely and chaste!" Francis praised, praised, praised. And the more he praised, the happier he became. For the one who sincerely praises is always a happy person. Should we speak of grudging praise, we are not really talking about praise at all but rather dealing with an unhappy, cramped person, a wizened, constrained, self-focused person. Praise breaks out of a joyous heart. Juan Diego naively says to our Lady in the story of Guadalupe, describing his wife, Maria Lucia, "Oh! I wish I could tell you! She was lovely, my Maria Lucia. I wish I could tell you. I wish you could know." Praise is inevitably gladly eager to share the charms, to tell the greatness, to describe the beauty of the beloved with others. Praise is humble. Praise is joyous.

Out of that flows its third characteristic. Praise is liberating. It takes us out of ourselves into the glory of another. It bursts open doors, breaks locks, sets us free. And this is what will be our occupation in heaven: forever expanding, being taken more and more out of even our own glorified selves into the glory of God. This alone offers evidence that praise is not static. Rather, of its nature it is dynamic. Praise breaks out. If we have lost our taste for praise, if we are "grudging" in our praise, if we see little to praise in others, then we shall certainly not see all that much to praise in God's higher creation either. We could be just as grudging about that. But, if we are praisers because we are humbly situated beneath the other whom in praise we are exalting, we shall be joyous, spontaneous, ungrudging, and eager, with eyes wide open to see all there is to be praised, liberated from the dank little dungeon of ourselves into the glory of another. It is in the glory of God and in the glory of others that we find ourselves. We do not find ourselves in self-focusedness, in constraint that only afflicts us with spiritual myopia. It is when we are liberated into God and into others, into praise of them, that we encounter our own true selves.

Turning those three characteristics around, we can examine together what tends to obscure them. The taste for praise is endangered or lost by self-absorption, the very opposite of humility, being always concerned with ourselves and ever, or at least a great part of the time, seeking our own exaltation. We are grieved if we are invited to attend to what is not praiseworthy and needs amending in ourselves. We take it amiss when this is pointed out by those whose duty it is to correct us and to help us see ourselves more clearly. We can make a great trauma out of things, excusing ourselves from effort because we are so self-absorbed. Then, of course, praise of God as well as of others is gravely endangered, if not forsaken, because humility lags and flags and sputters out in us.

Similarly, if there is fault-finding, then obviously

the joyousness of praise is afflicted. The fault-finder will always have his dark reward. We can find fault in any situation if we wish to do so because no human situation is perfect. If we set out to find fault with one another, we shall inevitably be rewarded, since everyone offers a field for this. And we can end this dark pursuit by finding fault with God. That may seem a stunning possibility at first, but do we not have to strike our breasts and admit that often enough we are grumbling at God, finding fault with God? Finding fault with God as well as others can become one's occupation. Thus is joyousness drained out of us and our darkness inflicted on others.

We can find fault with the sun because it is hot. It makes us uncomfortable in the summer. Instead, we could be standing with Saint Francis and praising the sun because it gives us the light of day. Our appreciation of God's most splendid creations can be dulled by fault-finding. Instead of rejoicing in the gorgeousness of the sunset, we can grumble that it is heralding the night and that light is going to die. We can find fault with God's greatest gifts, chafing at his grace because it invites us to transcend our present state and to expand our present narrow attitude. We can murmur at the inspiration to sacrifice because it demands something of us. Fault-finding comes from a heart that has lost the joyousness of praising.

Then, the opposite of that third characteristic of

praise—that it is liberating—can only be negativism. Just as with the positive attributes of praise, so with these three dark characteristics of the unpraising heart: we find them flowing out of one another into one another. This third property of the unpraising heart negativism, comes from self-absorption and fault-finding. We cannot have a positive enjoyment of flowers because they need to be watered, watched, picked. We need them for the altar and so they must be sheltered from the heat of the sun, be fertilized, be protected from infestation or blight. These needs, calling for one's energy, disaffect the negative person.

Saint Francis loved the flowers; Saint Clare said to her sisters, "Don't miss the trees!" Saint Vincent de Paul in his old age used to tap with his cane at the flowers as he walked in the garden and admonish them, "Don't shout so loud!" To him they were shouting the praises of God. It is the occupation of every Christian to praise all the works of God. Sad to say, we can gradually degenerate into the peevishness of the unpraising heart, because flowers have to be watered and tended and are such a lot of trouble, really.

We have an eternal vocation to praise God, and we practice for it on earth by praising him in all his ways which are not our ways, for his thoughts which are not our thoughts, in his wisdom which is beyond our understanding, for his plans which excel our comprehension, so that our taste for praising grows and grows.

It is the one who praises God in the small flower who will see an even smaller one to praise, just as it is the one who is grudging, negative, and self-absorbed who will see the flower either as something that merely demands tending or as something not worth seeing at all. This person will end up stepping on the flower in one way or another.

There are flowers blooming all about us: sentient, animate, human flowers. If we do not praise them in the love of our hearts, we will finish by stepping on them, too. And if we do that, how shall we ever grow in the praise of God? We rehearse for eternity every day. And this great *Anima Christi* prayer, as it comes to its climactic end, reveals to us what eternity is: the state where all the saints of God praise him forever and ever. We could approach that state with renewed vigor today. How many things there are for which to praise God! We are alive! God has loved us, thought of us, wanted us to live. May he be praised! What God is there like this God who thought of creating me? I am a unique thought of God! And God has redeemed us. May he be praised! Even after we have denied his grace, betrayed his inspirations again and again, disappointed him over and over, he still thinks us worth redeeming. May he be praised! And he made this day for us to live in and gave us others to love. Saint Francis walked about like one bemused, saying, "And then God gave me brothers!" May he be praised!

What do we hear as Saint Clare speaks her last words on this earth? "Be you praised, Lord, for having created me!" She is confiding to us what she had rehearsed carefully and long for eternity, so that now a whole life of praising God in all his works could only end with this great cry of praise. Not: Thank God, the pain is over now and death is going to put an end to it, and I am going to enter into heaven. Oh, no! This very sick woman, suffering in body and so long-suffering in spirit, too, cries out in praise. She is joyous, she is humble, she is liberated beyond what some of our modern liberated folk could even imagine. "Be you praised, Lord, for having created me!" The thing to do is daily to practice for eternity, where we hope with all the saints to praise him forever and ever.

XII

AMEN!

THUS WE ARRIVE AT THE END of our *Anima Christi* prayer. We come to "Amen", an extremely important word. We say it so often; and, unfortunately, we perhaps often say it lightly without much or any realization of the responsibility to which we commit ourselves with every "Amen" we utter. How often are we consciously aware that when we add our "Amen" to a prayer, we are making a solemn agreement to what the prayer puts forth? Some of the orations of the Church are really quite dangerous if we are not prepared to give what they are asking, approve by our manner of living what they are saying, assent in action to what they commit us. A blithe and half-thinking "Amen" can be signing us up to what we do not really intend to give. We have said by our "Amen": This I believe, this I will do, with this I agree. That is one consideration.

Another is this: just as all prayers are completed with their "Amen", so are our lives fulfilled in their "amens". In a sense, the "amens" of our lives are more important even than the *fiats* of our lives.

At the beginning of creation, there was uttered that great word of the Father to which we all thrill: "*Fiat!*" One would not need to be much of a poet or even to have much imagination to respond with a shiver of appreciation to that mighty *Fiat!* Let it be! *Fiat lux!* Let light be. And light was. And so through all of creation, including ours, thunders the mighty word. That great call of God, that agreement of God within himself that this thing should be. Each one of us is a *fiat* of God. He has said: Let him be, let her be. And he was. She was. Our dignity lies in being each of us a unique *fiat* of God. He desired me to be. And thus I was and am and ever will be. My personal life consists, or should consist, of a continual encircling of that initial devine *Fiat!* with my own life's chorale of *fiats*. It is, after all, quite up to me whether I live my life as a sonata of self-elected *fiats* to God's unfolding will for me, or as a cacophony of dissonant rejections.

That mighty *Fiat* is returned and re-echoed to us in the lovely *Fiat* of our Lady at the Annunciation. She takes the great creative word of God, and, understanding dimly and yet somehow clearly (she knew the Scriptures well), she responds to it, making it her own. She commits herself to be the handmaid of the Lord in all of his plans for her. *Fiat!* Let it be! Be it done unto me.

Again we have the *Fiat* of the God–Man in the Incarnation, those words that present themselves as the dedication of Christ's autobiography: "I have come to do your will, O my God." That the Father's will to redeem the world should be done, Christ speaks his own *Fiat* at the beginning of his human existence, agreeing to take upon himself all our sins, all our guilt, all our misery, all our need. As the Scriptures so poignantly put it, "the chastisement that made us whole" (Is 53:5). To all of this, in the Incarnation, Jesus says: "*Fiat!*"

But back to the great *Fiat* of the eternal Father in creation. So grand, so moving, the beginning of all that is, the beginning of us! But does it not fill us with terror to think what would have happened if God had not constantly, repeatedly, said "Amen!" to his *Fiat* of creation? If he had said, "Let the light be! Let the land be! Let the waters form! Let the sky be!" and had not gone on fueling the light, sustaining the matter, holding up the sky? Or if his great *Fiat* of each of us had not been followed by his continual sustaining "Amen" of us? What if he had not maintained us in all our times of personal weakness? In our personal history, our behavioral patterns, our failures, our weaknesses that tend to unravel his great creative *Fiat*, when we did not respond to the ideal of his creative *Fiat* of us into glory—suppose God had not gone on pronouncing his "Amen" of us? To speak in our impoverished human language, which is, after all, the only language we have, it would be as though God demanded: "But what have they done with my *Fiat* of them?"

Every day of our lives, every hour, every moment, the Father has to say "Amen" to his *Fiat* of us. Otherwise, we would not be. It is not enough for God to have said: "*Fiat*", and then set creation adrift. One says with utmost reverence that God has to be true to his own *Fiat* with his own continuing "Amen". And so do we.

For our blessed Savior, it had to be more than the resounding, "I come to do your will, O my God!" To save men by taking on their guilt, their ingratitude, their limitedness, their dreariness, their drabness, their infidelities. What would have been the God-Man's *Fiat* of redemption if he had not uttered "Amen!" to it in every suffering year of his suffering life? It can be very fruitful to search the Scriptures with that in mind. If we look for the "Amens" of Jesus, we shall find that they abound. One thinks almost immediately of that episode with the ten lepers, where our Lord revealed his human heart to us in such an intimate way, allowing us to witness his hurt at the ingratitude of the nine. "Were not ten made clean? Where are the nine?" (Lk 17:17). He is saying: I am hurt. Where are they? Why do they not bother to thank me? But then, by continuing his ministry of healing, he said a new "Amen!"

Again, when he said his *Fiat* to taking on the burden of our dullness, he had to fulfill it in many "Amens". "King! King! King!" shouts the dull-eyed crowd, looking for easy bread (Jn 6:15). Make him king! We get bread without working! And Jesus ran away to pray alone, not because he did not want to be king, but because he knew what was in their dull hearts so like our own. He was to say another time that, indeed, he was a king. "For this was I born, and for this I have come into the world" (Jn 18:37). But it was only a handy breadwinner, even bread-maker, that the crowd wanted. Nor could they have dreamed that this, too, he would one day be: himself their bread. But he came down from the mountain, back to the crowds. He said another "Amen!" to our dullness.

When he said to Philip, "Have I been with you so long, and yet you do not know me, Philip?" (Jn 14:9), was Jesus not saying an "Amen!" to the Father's *Fiat* of Philip, with all Philip's limitations, so well known to us in our own selves? Our blessed Savior was fulfilling his redemptive *Fiat* to taking on all the limitations of weak and sinful men. And very notably at the Last Supper there was wrung an agonizing "Amen!" from his disappointed heart, when his own little community made so poor a response. If it is true that there was still much they did not understand, it is likewise true that there was a great deal that they did understand. They did not realize that he was about to enter into his agony. They did not understand that he was about to be crucified, even though he had tried to tell them. But they did surely understand that this was the most solemn feast of the year. They did know that the Master had made very special arrangements for this liturgy with them. They certainly realized that this was a most precious and intimate hour with him. And what were they doing? Squabbling with one another about who should be preferred to the other, who should be first. And so Jesus says a mighty "Amen!" to his redemptive *Fiat*. Undefeated by their pettiness, he utters his silent "Amen!"—down on the floor, at their feet. In the end, he will love them into martyrdom by his indefatigable "amens" to the Father's creative *Fiat* of them, and his own redemptive *Fiat*.

And our Lady's *Fiat* at the Annunciation? Let it be! I am his handmaid. But what a lifetime of "amens" had to follow upon that splendid hour and that glorious *Fiat*! To what avail the heart-shaking *Fiat* of her initial surrender if she had not uttered the suffering "amens" of all the years that followed? Certain incidents stand out at once. That time in the temple when the Scriptures tell us that she did not understand (Lk 2:50). She had to utter a very suffering "Amen" to being a handmaid then. A handmaid of God content to go on serving without understanding what he was doing, what he was saying, or why. She had to say

134

"Amen!" to her *Fiat* when he left her for his public life. And how many "amens" when she stood on the fringes of the crowd? She was required to say her own agonizing "Amen!" when he entered into his Passion, and how often before that in the prefiguring agonies of his life in the town? When they tried to throw him over the brow of the hill. When they spoke of him with such sneering condescension. What an "Amen!" she uttered in the silence of her heart when she did not try to restrain him on the Way of his Cross. Under the Cross, Mary had come a lifetime of "amens" from that hour of her girlhood when she spoke her first beautiful *Fiat!*

Tradition tells us that our Lady lived seventy-two years on earth. That left her a long time to be without him. That marks out a long, long refrain of "amens". Her glorious Assumption and reunion with her divine Son was the climax not only of her initial *Fiat!* but of all her "amens" as well. And it was God's final "Amen!" upon both.

Then, too, we do have some particular *fiats* of our own. Those of us who are professed religious have said the mighty *Fiat* of our vowed life. Let this be!—that I be given to a life of obedience, of chastity, of poverty. *Fiat* is the great word of our Profession just as it is the word of marriage vows and, indeed, of every sincere and determined dedication. Let it be!—this total surrender that involves a whole lifetime of effort and striving. Yet it is possible to say that same grand word: *Fiat*, let it be, in just the opposite sense. Do we not sometimes say, "Oh, let it be." And we mean: Just forget about it, don't bother about it, what's the difference anyhow? Just let it go, let it slide. Let it be. Is that not exactly what we do when our noble and positive *fiats* are not followed by "amens"?

Looking back in review of all our considerations on this great prayer, *Anima Christi*, we see that we have dealt with a *fiat* to each one. We do want this to be: that the animating principle of Christ might rule my life; that I might gather strength and be saved by the body of Christ; be inebriated with the blood of Christ; desire to give everything with the same utterness and finality with which that sacred water came from his side. And so on through every reflection until now we say together: "Amen!" It is a very large responsibility we assume by saying "Amen!" to the imperatives of the *Anima Christi*. But if it is not said and lived, to what purpose the reflection? The "Amen" of every day must speak the truth of our *Fiat*. There is much required for a *fiat*. And yet, *fiat* is really easier to say than "amen". For every *fiat* requires hosts of "amens" to be complete.

Saint Francis said "Amen!" so well. He was called to do great things in the Church, far greater than he knew when he first raced out to gather stones to "repair a church falling into ruins". *Fiat* was the burning word of his first response. But then there came the years of "amens" when unfaithful sons broke his great heart, when so many were not true to his ideal, when the purpose of his life and his foundation seemed confounded. And he uttered each one. Again, with Saint Clare, our hearts thrill to the vision of the lovely young girl running off to elope with Christ, singing out a lyric *Fiat!* to all she leaves behind and turning toward an unknown future. But she had to bear the consequences of that *Fiat* and verify it with a long lifetime of "amens". We can search her brief writings for her "amens", and we shall find them on the lines and between the lines until the great final "Amen!" on her deathbed.

We all thrill to *"Fiat!"* while tending to become all too unthinking about the "Amen!" If we could really see our "amens" for what they are, see the unfolding occasions in our life as completing and authenticating our *fiat*, our lives would perhaps be very different.

The Eternal Father is at this moment authenticating his creative *Fiat* of us by sustaining us in creation. The Son is at this moment in his forgiveness authenticating his redemptive *Fiat*. Our Lady, by keeping her motherhood of men, is authenticating her *Fiat*. And we need to authenticate ours. *Amen.*